THE PHILOSOPHY
OF PRIMARY EDUCATION

The Students Library of Education

THE PHILOSOPHY
OF PRIMARY EDUCATION

An Introduction

by

R. F. DEARDEN

Lecturer in the Philosophy of Education,
University of London Institute of Education

LONDON

ROUTLEDGE & KEGAN PAUL

NEW YORK: HUMANITIES PRESS

First published 1968
by Routledge & Kegan Paul Ltd
Broadway House, 68–74 Carter Lane
London, E.C.4
Reprinted 1968
Reprinted (twice) 1969
Printed in Great Britain
by Butler & Tanner Limited
Frome and London
Library of Congress Catalog Card Number 68-21589
SBN 7100 4223 x (c)
SBN 7100 6648 1 (p)

372.942
D 285 p

THE STUDENTS LIBRARY OF EDUCATION has been designed to meet the needs of students of Education at Colleges of Education and at University Institutes and Departments. It will also be valuable to practising teachers and educationalists. The series takes full account of the latest developments in teacher-training and of new methods and approaches in education. Separate volumes will provide authoritative and up-to-date accounts of the topics within the major fields of sociology, philosophy and history of education, educational psychology and method. Care has been taken that specialist topics are treated lucidly and usefully for the non-specialist reader. Altogether the Students Library of Education will provide a comprehensive introduction and guide to anyone concerned with the study of education, and with educational theory and practice.

J. W. TIBBLE

THE FIELD OF PRIMARY EDUCATION is one in which countless gifted and dedicated teachers are engaged. Their thought about what they are doing, however, and their attempts to convey the secret of their success to others, has never done justice to their practice. Indeed the theory of primary education is more studded with slogans arising from an unexamined ideology than any other. The Plowden Report recently centred public interest and concern on this area; but the attempts at theory which informed some of the thinking of the Report lacked clarity, argument, and often empirical support. The time is indeed ripe for a thorough examination of the assumptions on which primary education is and should be based.

Mr Dearden is in an admirable position to conduct such an examination. He was a primary teacher himself for eight years, during which time he obtained a first-class degree in philosophy in his spare time and a distinction in the Diploma in Education. He therefore brings to this field of education a rare combination—extensive practical experience and rigorous thinking of a philosophical sort about the theoretical foundations of practice. His approach is both critical and constructive. Not everybody will accept his conclusions, but at least the issues are sharpened so that those who take his arguments seriously will be able to work out more clearly where they stand. This book should prove to be a landmark in the history of educational theory; for there has been no such previous comprehensive attempt to tackle the assumptions of primary education by an educationalist well versed in the techniques of modern philosophy.

RICHARD PETERS

CONTENTS

PREFACE

'Free and indiscriminate use of words such as discovery has led some critics to the view that English primary education needs to be more firmly based on closely argued educational theory . . . What is immediately needed is that teachers should bring to bear on their day to day problems astringent intellectual scrutiny.' (Plowden Report, 1967, para. 550.)

It must be confessed that there is little in the theoretical literature on English primary education that could fairly be called 'astringent intellectual scrutiny'. All too often what one finds are doctrinal enthusiasms liberally laced with little stories about what Sandra, or Jonathan, or Josephine did, and how deeply satisfying it was. In so far as any awareness of a possible objector is shown at all, he is often something of a caricature created by a polarized emotional reaction against 'formal teachers'. The ratio of assertion to argument is, therefore, as one would expect, extremely high, with little interest shown in gaining a critical or discriminating acceptance of what is asserted. That is why 'doctrinal enthusiasm' seems so apt a description for it.

Certainly the situation is one that badly calls for improvement, and for some greater token of respect for even quite ordinary standards of argument. This book does at least attempt to provide some 'astringent intellectual scrutiny', more especially of such central theoretical concepts as those of need, interest, growth, play, experience, activity and self-expression. The book also seeks to make a contribution towards getting a 'closely argued educational theory', in so far as something essentially interdisciplinary like educational theory can be closely argued from one point of view only, namely that of the philosophy of education. Psychological and sociological commentaries, and historical and comparative perspectives, are also relevant to educational theory, yet today no-one can hope adequately to compass all of them. Still, if anyone ought to be prepared to stick his neck out a little here, one would have thought it ought to be the philosopher, so perhaps there is some excuse.

Yet a sceptic might well ask how there could be a philosophy of *primary* education—for surely there is just education, the demarcation of a primary stage in the process being due only to psychological and to administrative considerations? There is much truth in this, as is recognized by the generality of the first parts of chapter four, on the curriculum. But since 1931 the primary school has, at least in recommendation, existed as a separate institution with its own ethos and interests. There has been developed a body of theory with particular reference to the primary stage, and it is with this theory that the philosophy of primary education is especially concerned. In this connection, mention might be made of the rather inexact phrases 'elementary school tradition' and 'child-centred theorist', both of which I use repeatedly. They are intended as general and schematic descriptive phrases. Any more specific and precise meaning that they are made to bear will, I venture to hope, be clear enough from the particular contexts of discussion in which they occur.

The book falls fairly evenly into two parts. The first part tries, by a long critical argument, to establish certain general aims and culminates in a positive suggestion as to what the curriculum ought, in general outline, to be. The second part is more concerned with the procedures of learning and teaching appropriate to such a curriculum, and here philosophical and general psychological issues are much more difficult to keep separate, since much of the argument has the philosophy of mind as its philosophical background. A plentiful sprinkling of references is provided in the body of the text, not so much out of a crushing sense of obligation to acknowledge every possible source of which I am conscious, though obviously there are proprieties to be observed here, as to give a detailed indication at every stage of how this introduction might be followed up by some further reading. In addition, some general suggestions for further reading are given at the end.

Mention of acknowledgements would be grossly incomplete, however, without a general expression of indebtedness to Professor R. S. Peters, of the University of London Institute of Education, and Professor P. H. Hirst, of King's College, London. Professor Peters has greatly helped me to a better understanding of ethics, the philosophy of mind and the possible bearings of both of these on education. To Professor Hirst I am mainly indebted for his seminal work on forms of knowledge and the curriculum. Most philosophers have, of course, had views on the forms of knowledge, for example Kant among the great and S. E. Toulmin among the more recent. But it was Professor Hirst who first excited me with the idea of tracing the possible curricular implications of such epistemological distinctions. For the detailed working out of this idea in relation to the primary school, however, I am alone responsible. Fortunately, the views of both Professor Peters and of Professor Hirst are now published, so that where I am indebted to them, my indebtedness is not only acknowledged but also manifest. In some places I have also drawn on previously published work of my own, but where this is so the material has all been re-worked specifically for the purposes of the present book.

In connection with the writing and preparation, I am especially grateful to Professor Peters for his interest, encouragement, detailed criticisms and valiant attempts to remedy my more deplorable lapses from good style. My wife also is to be thanked for the labour of detection and deciphering involved in typing out my manuscript and so making it into something which others also could read.

Chapter One

THE CHANGING CONCEPT OF THE PRIMARY SCHOOL

THE ELEMENTARY SCHOOL TRADITION

The primary school came into existence with the appearance of the first of the three Hadow Reports, *The Education of the Adolescent* (H.M.S.O., 1926). As one can see from the title of that report, the primary school came into existence as a consequence of interests which lay elsewhere, namely with children of what would now be called secondary age. With the school leaving age then at fourteen, and at least three years thought to be necessary for a recognizable secondary course, a break was seen to be indicated at the age of eleven. The choice of this age also fitted in well with the already existing age of transfer of the 'scholarship' children to what are now called the grammar schools. This took place at eleven.

Thus the 'all-age' elementary schools were, at least in recommendation, split at eleven into primary and secondary schools, though the actual reorganization was still not complete thirty years later. By 'primary' school, however, the second Hadow Report meant only the school for children of from seven to eleven, the 'juniors', since the infant schools for the five-to-sevens were often already separate departments, defined by their being prior to 'standard one'. But in this book, 'primary school' will be taken to include both infant and junior schools, or Plowden's first and middle schools, and thus covers the period of compulsory education from five up to eleven or twelve years of age.

The general character of the all-age elementary schools, however, had been formed in the last half of the nineteenth century. This period saw some thirty years of the notorious system of 'payment by results', following Lowe's Code of 1862 for 'popular education'. Even when the forces which formed that general character ceased to operate, it proved to be stubbornly self-perpetuating, and the liberal proposals for the primary school of the second and third Hadow Reports, published in 1931 and 1933, were slow to gain ground. This was especially so in the 'junior' departments, in which the recommendations of 1931 had still had only little effect by 1948 (H.M.S.O., 1952, prefatory note).

This slowness was due partly to concentration on secondary re-organization and building, partly to the 'scholarship' examination at eleven, which more or less replaced payment-by-results in encouraging the view that the primary school's justification lay solely in preparing children for the secondary school, and partly also it was due to the sheer inertia of a by now well-established tradition (H.M.S.O., 1952, ch. 1). Only gradually did the infant departments free themselves from a similar subordination to the needs of the juniors.

Indeed, a discerning eye can still detect many of the features characteristic of the elementary schools at the turn of the century. The 'eleven plus' is still commonly referred to as the 'scholarship' examination. Age groups are still sometimes called 'standards'. There still exist in places a reverence for registers and an awe of the inspector. Headteachers may still sometimes be required to gain the approval of 'the office' for the most trivial and detailed matters, and insist on a similar subordination from their staff. Yet if changes have come slowly, the infant schools for the five-to seven-year-olds have now substantially transformed themselves, and in the last decade even the junior schools have abandoned some of their traditions and much of their old ethos.

These, of course, are historical rather than philosophical considerations, but it will prove useful in the later sections of this book to have a rough model in mind of the general character of the elementary school tradition. It provides the point of departure for change, and is the background of existing practice against which successive reformers are inveighing and which often determines the form of their protest. It therefore deserves some further elaboration, even if only of a very generalised and schematic kind.

The curriculum of the elementary school was dominated by the criterion of social utility. As W. A. C. Stewart puts it: 'It is a truism to say that the elementary school system of the nineteenth century was not primarily intended to have any cultural value but was predominantly and unmistakably utilitarian' (Mannheim and Stewart, 1962, 21). Since the institution was also predominantly a working class one, 'social utility' can be further specified as 'what it is useful to teach the sons and daughters of the working classes'.

Principally, of course, this meant the teaching of the three R's: reading, writing and arithmetic. It was thought useful that these children should be able to read, be able to write neatly, legibly and with correct spelling and punctuation, and be quick and accurate in the main departments of the social applications of arithmetic, such as number, money, weight, length, capacity and time. In addition to these 'basic skills', a certain amount of factual material came also to be included, so that something of the geography of the British Isles and British Empire was learned, a suitably patriotic view of our national history was formed, and some facts about certain biological phenomena were learned. Very important also was a knowledge of the Bible. One of the original impulses behind teaching these children to read was that they should be able to read the Bible for themselves.

In addition to the criterion of social utility, there was also operative a demand that this schooling should be cheap, so that mass instruction to fifty or sixty or even many more was very common. The general pattern was for a lesson to be delivered and then to be followed up by drills, practices, catechisms, tests and revisions, with uniform standards of attainment for all, and success achieved if evidence of adequate memorization could be shown. What was taught might not have been understood, but the important thing was, as it were, to know the words in order to be saved. Even with the introduction of 'art and craft' into the curriculum, the same general pattern of instruction and drill prevailed. Fifty careful copies of a picture, classroom object or blackboard model would be produced for art, or a long series of graded exercises, culminating perhaps in the manufacture of a paper envelope, would serve for craft. Social utility and cheapness ruled here as elsewhere. Certainly there was no room for 'mere play'. Children came to school to work, and the teacher had to see that that was what they did. There could be no place for anything as time-wasting and trivial as play, apart from some brief intermissions as minimal concessions which had to be made to animal spirits.

Inevitably, the ethos of the elementary school was authoritarian, and the authority of the teacher over the children was marked in many ways. He was physically separate from and raised above his class, facing them from a dais or high chair. The children were required to observe various rituals of respect, such as prompt standing up on the appearance of authority-figures, speech richly punctuated with 'sir' and 'miss', procedures for gaining permission to move, or indeed to do anything, procedures for gaining the teacher's attention, and so on. A teacher who successfully exacted such observances was a 'good disciplinarian'. His children did not talk, fidget, waste time or do anything of their own accord; they listened, and obediently did as they were told, waiting when they had done it for further instructions.

This authoritarianism was reinforced in many ways. The content of what was taught was made dependent for its acceptability on having come from the appropriate authority, whether the teacher or the class textbook, so that the decision-procedure in all cases of doubt or ignorance was to ask the teacher and be told. 'Teacher says' settled the matter, and it was a shameful thing, to be concealed at all costs, for the teacher not to know or not to be able to say. One learned in response to such directions as 'look at the blackboard', 'watch how I do it', 'repeat after me' and 'do as I say'. Again, the expected reluctance of children to learn necessitated a system of incentives to work sustained in effectiveness by the pressure of the teacher. Competition for stars, places of prestige, points and privileges lured on the co-operative, while the rest were goaded by threats, penalties and punishments of many kinds, from sitting with hands on heads or kneeling on the floor to being isolated in some cupboard or corner, or given the cane.

The teachers and headteachers stood similarly subordinated and receptive towards the acts and decisions of yet higher authorities, whose regulations sought to secure that the utilitarian aims of the school would be achieved, and that neither money nor minutes would be wasted in the process. W. A. L. Blyth comments on the elementary school that 'most of its teachers were themselves too limited in ability and in education and too insecure both financially and socially to be able to conceive of their task in terms other than those of meticulous and conscientious compliance with the routines that they knew' (Blyth, 1965, II, 27).

The authoritarianism institutionally required from the teacher was not, of course, without its recognizable effects on the teacher's own personality, as Waller made clear in a section of his book called 'What Teaching does to Teachers', though he was referring to the parallel system in America (Waller, 1932). For a vivid literary portrayal of the transformation required in a person as a condition of success in the elementary school, one might turn to chapter thirteen of D. H. Lawrence's novel *The Rainbow*, where a young girl, Ursula, is given a post in such a school. She saw:

all the schoolteachers, drudging unwillingly at the graceless task of compelling many children into one disciplined, mechanical set, reducing the whole set to an automatic state of obedience and attention, and then of commanding their acceptance of various pieces of knowledge. The first great task was to reduce sixty children to one state of mind, or being. This state of mind must be produced automatically, through the will of the teacher, and the will of the whole school authority, imposed upon the will of the children. The point was that the headmaster and the teachers should have one will in authority, which should bring the will of the children into accord.

But it was not all gloom, and Lawrence himself captures the elementary school classroom in one of its more rewarding moments in his poem *The Best of School*.

TWO FORMATIVE INFLUENCES

At this point one might pause for a moment to reflect on these generalizations about the elementary school tradition and to try to identify the formative influences at work in producing it. Two such important influences can be picked out for brief comment. The first of these, as with any system of educational practice, relates to social structure in its economic and social class aspects. It has already been mentioned that the dominant criterion for curriculum content was social utility, and that 'utility' meant what was useful for working-class children to learn and could cheaply be provided for them. The stress on 'basic skills' and the narrow way in which these were conceived were the educational counterpart to a range of adult occupations which called for factory workers, shop assistants, low-grade clerical workers and, very important for the girls, domestic servants. As well as the limited knowledge which such occupations required there were also certain attitudes, notably an attitude of suitable deference towards social superiors. Substantial change in the primary schools has come only with change in this particular formative influence, though the education of the very youngest children was already freeing itself from it at the time of the Hadow Reports.

Today, as everyone knows, the pattern and character of occupations is rapidly changing. The equipment of narrow skills drilled into elementary school children would no longer be adequate, or even sometimes necessary, as more and more low-grade work is mechanized. Increasingly, firms prefer to give their own particular kinds of training. Increasingly, also, jobs require a theoretical ingredient, not just a practical know-how to be gained simply by long apprenticeship. Employers look to the schools for a general education which will produce people who are adaptable and flexible (Plowden Report, paras. 494–6) and 'adaptability' is as much a function of having general concepts and principles at one's command as it is of an attitude of readiness to try something different. Not surprisingly, therefore, mathematics and science are at the forefront of the minds of those who now call for a 'general education'. Doubtless much of the impetus and the financial encouragement for the current changes in mathematics teaching in primary schools, and for the introduction of elementary science, spring from this economic demand.

This and other similar changes in the content of the curriculum have repercussions on general methodology, of course, since they call for insight, understanding and critical acceptance: features which consort ill with any authoritarianism. Indeed, advocates of these curricular and methodological changes have often been quite conscious of the fact that what they were recommending was incompatible with the attitudes going along with a general authoritarianism. Max Wertheimer, for example, explicitly linked his 'productive thinking' with democracy and the dignity of man. When insightful methods of learning are used 'an attitude is implied on his part, a willingness to face problems straight, a readiness to follow them up courageously and sincerely. . . . This, I think, is one of the great attributes that constitute the dignity of man' (Wertheimer, 1945, 243). Not surprisingly, therefore, we find movement away from the elementary school tradition occurring not only in consequence of economic change, but also in consequence of wider social and political changes.

Against the view that a cheap and suitably inferior kind of training was good enough for the children of the working classes, there developed a political movement demanding 'education for all' and 'equality of opportunity'. At first, these demands were satisfied by opening up the 'secondary' (later grammar) schools to an increasing number of children who had demonstrated their merits in an examination at the age of eleven. By 1944, social justice demanded that *all* the places in the grammar schools be given on grounds of merit, and none be reserved for children whose only merit was having parents who could afford the fees. But such changes were made within a framework of assumptions which included an acceptance of social class structure as something that was given, a *datum*. Granted that assumption, heredity was seen as the principal factor in determining variations in ability, and selection and streaming were seen as efficient means of doing justice to the then given abilities.

However, once the existing social class structure was no longer automatically accepted as part of the nature of things, it was quickly revealed as itself being a major factor in determining variations in ability, and the school was seen as a possible agency through which one might deliberately compensate for certain inequalities of opportunity, namely those arising from the varying attitudes shown to children, and the variable provision and encouragement given to them, by different social classes. The movements against eleven-plus selection, against streaming, and now for positive discrimination in favour of certain socially depressed areas (Plowden Report, ch. 5), stemmed largely from the trend of this wider social and political thinking. Much of the acrimony and mutual misunderstanding which have accompanied these actual and recommended changes, one may surmise, are due to the fact that some have come to see as variables, subject to human choice and control, what for others still lies beyond the horizon of human agency, as something given, fixed, part of the nature of things, and perhaps even conveniently so if in fact it works to their own advantage.

But besides the influence of social structure in its economic and social class aspects, one may see also in the elementary school tradition a second influence at work, and one which is not wholly unrelated to the first. This second influence is that of a certain theory of human nature deriving from religion. According to this theory, children are to be seen as being by nature bad. That is to say, their spontaneous impulses are to be distrusted, they cannot see what is true or good for themselves, and hence they stand in need of a redemption which in practice can only be gained by obedience to adult authority. One should therefore distrust spontaneity, independence, or self-direction in children. Such things are sensed to be the potentially anarchic symptoms of a self-will that must be curbed, and in some cases broken. Hence the plethora of such proverbs and sayings as 'spare the rod and spoil the child', or 'Satan will find mischief for idle hands to do'. The implications of this for the teacher fitted in very well with the utilitarian demand for efficiency, and with the general ethos of authoritarianism engendered on the one hand by the methods of mass instruction, and on the other hand by the administrative and social hierarchy. Children should be directed in all that they do, told in detail what to do and how to do it, kept busy, and trained in obedience to such directions. Not only was the good disciplinarian giving secular instruction and instilling appropriately deferential attitudes, but he was also making his contribution towards the saving of souls.

A feature of this theory of human nature deserving of remark is its self-confirming character. That is to say, if one does in fact believe children to be by nature bad, and if one makes institutional arrangements of the kind described to combat this badness, then what happens abundantly confirms one's expectations. Bad children will be reluctant to learn, and so it turns out. Bad children will laugh if the teacher's dignity is momentarily upset, and so they do. They will relax and fight if control is withdrawn, and they will erupt into wildness when the pressures are off, all of which is confirmed.

Furthermore, accounts of different regimes in which none of these things are noticeably present will be received with incredulity. Knowing questions will be asked about what such children do when so-and-so, and any news of a need for some control or direction will be received with relief. And no doubt such suspicions and reluctance to believe will in some cases be justified, for belief in the badness of children polarizes in some people an opposite belief in their natural goodness, so that authoritarianism may be countered by sentimentality. Dewey saw the mechanism of this style of reaction very clearly when he said that 'in spite of itself any movement that thinks and acts in terms of an 'ism becomes so involved in reaction against other 'isms that it is unwittingly controlled by them. For it then forms its principles by reaction against them instead of by a comprehensive, constructive survey of actual needs, problems and possibilities' (Dewey, 1938, Preface). One thesis of this book will be that much of the child-centred reaction against the authoritarianism of the elementary-school tradition has been controlled in this way.

CHANGE AND UNCERTAINTY

The elementary-school tradition had at least one virtue. It made clear to the teacher what he was supposed to do, arranged a concerted programme of mutually supportive teaching, and provided institutional backing for such measures as the teacher had to take. With the eclipse of that tradition, the concept of the primary school has, perhaps only temporarily, become somewhat clouded. There are, of course, those who talk approvingly of 'good teachers', 'good practice' and 'good learning situations', as if what was 'good' just *showed* itself, and as clearly and unambiguously to all as does what is tall, or square, or four-footed. The evaluative 'good', however, implies criteria which, characteristically, are somewhat naïvely taken for granted. Yet to take such criteria for granted, and not to become conscious of or to examine them, is precisely what one cannot do in times of change, when traditional practices are being brought wholesale into question and reforms of doubtlessly genuine value are intermixed with gimmickry and hobby-horses. It is precisely the general evaluative criteria of what is 'good' which need attention if the constant flood of recommendations and of advice from all sides is to be sifted, assessed and intelligently adapted to local circumstances, and if a coherent and concerted programme of activities for a school is to be evolved.

We can all see that reforms are needed, and badly overdue in many junior schools particularly, but what is less clear is which reforms are needed. Economic, social and political changes beyond the control of individual teachers, or even of the teaching profession, have, over the course of a quarter of a century, made the break up of the elementary school tradition inevitable. But what is not inevitable is the detailed shape of the educational practices which will now emerge. At this level, even the individual teacher has some degree of autonomy and can be a constructive, formative influence.

How should he conceive of his role in the new primary schools? Is he to be an instructor, an unobtrusive arranger of self-directed activities, a therapist, a guarantor of happiness, an engineer of warm personal relationships in which none shall feel the draught of disapproval? What is he to teach, if indeed he may 'teach' at all without suffering the pangs of a conscience bred in him by an extreme child-centred ideology? Is ignorance in children acceptable so long as good attitudes go along with it? Does arithmetical computation matter any more? Are mis-spelling and mis-shapen handwriting any longer to be a stimulus to correction, or is it enough that the child has 'expressed' himself? Do most things 'just come' if only materials are spread around and everyone is smiled at, continuously? Are there still naughty children who would benefit by a sharp word or a smack, or does even the thought that this may be so simply betray the latent sadism of one's nature and one's lamentable ignorance of psychology? Are subjects, time-tables and schemes of work to be dismissed as arbitrary fictions, unnatural and quite foreign to the child, while instead growth is to be observed and interests are to be noted?

These are far from being unreal questions, and in the following chapters we shall have to examine a number of the theories which lie behind them to see how much that is acceptable can be extracted from them, and what aspects of them call for criticism. In so far as a positive and constructive view emerges from this critical scrutiny, it will be seen to be neither a reactionary advocacy of authoritarianism, nor an enthusiastic centring of everything on 'the child'. Rather, it will follow Dewey's advice when he said that 'those who are looking ahead to a new movement in education, adapted to the existing need for a new social order, should think in terms of Education itself rather than in terms of some 'ism about education, even such an 'ism as "progressivism" ' (Dewey, 1938, Preface). But as is often the case with Dewey, he is being rather cryptic here.

Chapter Two

AIMS (1): NEEDS AND INTERESTS

The elementary school tradition stressed knowledge and skills that would be useful to adult life, though it was readily conceded that such knowledge and skill might be of little interest to children at the time they acquired it. For this reason, and for others mentioned in the previous chapter, the elementary school was authoritarian in its ethos, with most of the pressure to work coming from the teacher, aided by various systems of artificial incentives. In reaction against this whole regime, many reformers went to the other extreme, just as Dewey pointed out that they would. They advocated 'starting from the child', a theme upon which there are very many variations.

Nevertheless, in no system of education can the teacher escape responsibility for the direction which things take. Even for the teacher to withdraw as much as possible from the scene is for him to make a choice. He is choosing an environment in which there will be no direction or explicit guidance, and hence he remains responsible for all that happens in consequence of that choice. Having a view as to which possible consequences are desirable and which not, or to put it another way, having a view as to what the *aims* of education ought to be, is therefore inescapable, even if that view is one which calls for non-intervention or withdrawal on the part of the teacher.

'Starting from the child', therefore, is not a policy that can dispense with having a view about aims, even though explicit mention and defence of them may be noticeably absent in such talk. The concepts associated with such a policy which do seem to come nearest to an explicit statement of aims, however, are those of need, interest, and growth, each of which deserves separate and close examination. In this chapter need and interest will be discussed, while growth is so complex a notion that a separate chapter will be necessary even to begin to unravel some of its strands. Attention to the concept of 'aim' itself will be delayed until chapter four.

NEEDS

Statements of 'need' abound in educational writing. One of the most recent examples relevant to primary education is to be found in *Primary Education in Scotland* (H.M.S.O., 1965), the first chapter of which is not, as one might reasonably have expected it to be, devoted to setting out aims, but rather gives a statement of the 'needs of the child', which are apparently five in number. Furthermore, this statement of needs concludes a chapter the character of which is almost purely psychological, so that one is led to suppose that if one wants to know what children need, then it is to psychology that one ought appropriately to turn. Empirical research will show the way, or so it is implied.

There are, however, two serious defects in any attempt to by-pass a discussion of aims by furnishing statements of need instead. The first of these defects relates to the logical impossibility of passing from statements of psychological fact to value-based judgements about what one ought to do. The second defect concerns some hidden assumptions behind thinking, as indeed is often thought, that an education which starts from the 'needs of the child' will solve the problem of motivation. Each of these defects merits some further elaboration, though for a more fully developed discussion, with due qualifications added, one would have to look elsewhere (see Komisar, 1961, or Dearden, 1966).

The first defect, then, concerns the attractiveness of the apparently empirical, or observationally based, character of statements of need. And indeed, on the face of it at least, needs-statements are simply empirical. If someone says that teachers need a salary increase of three hundred pounds per year, or that students need at least two advanced levels to enter university, or that owners of dogs need a licence, is it not simply a matter of fact that this is so?

If one had occasion actually to make a categorical assertion of the form '*x* needs *y*', would it not simply be a matter of fact that *x* had not already got *y*, and furthermore that getting *y* would indeed achieve whatever results were regarded as desirable of achievement. Surely these would be matters of fact, and some appropriate method of fact-finding, whether ordinary observation or sophisticated research, would be not just relevant but absolutely indispensable. The catch, however, lies in the implication of there being a condition desirable of achievement; for this brings to light the *valuational* basis of needs-statements, and the necessary subservience of the empirical data to such values.

Teachers *need* an increase of three hundred pounds only if it is a good thing to have one's salary so advanced. Students *need* two advanced levels only if going to university is regarded as something desirable, or worthwhile. Owners of dogs *need* a licence only because the law backs with an obligation the desirability of having one. Simply that someone does not actually have something, or that he would have to have it *if* he wanted to do something else, does not establish a need. Teachers do not have classes of seventy children, but no-one will therefore detect a *need* here. Yet if we thought mass instruction a good thing, as it was thought to be in one phase of the elementary school tradition, then we might well say that classes of seventy were needed. Confronted with statements of need, then, it is appropriate to inquire into the valuational basis of such statements. What values are being assumed here? What is being assumed to be desirable? And to see this is to see through the merely apparent empirical character of needs-statements. It is also to see that psychology, or indeed any other empirical science, logically must fail at some point as a sufficient warrant for asserting something to be needed.

Of course, often there is wide and proper agreement as to what is valuable, or desirable, or obligatory, and against a background of such consensus it is the researcher who has the important points to make. Thus when Bowlby claimed to have found, and let us assume for the sake of discussion that it really was there to be found, that maternal deprivation in early childhood caused an 'affectionless' character to be formed, then he was warranted in asserting the need of maternal care in childhood, for we all agree that being an 'affectionless' character is *undesirable*.

But we do not always agree over what is desirable. The child-centred reformers did not agree with the architects of the elementary tradition over what was desirable. In such circumstances, it is simply begging the question to talk about needs, or to pretend that there is nothing at issue that cannot be settled by empirical research. One has to look behind statements of need to the values that are guiding them, for it is here that the issue substantially lies. Defenders of the elementary school tradition could, with perfect propriety, talk of the 'needs of the child'. On their view, the needs of the child would be to pay attention and to listen, to do as he was told and then wait for further instructions, to show obedience and respect towards adults in authority, and so on. What was *desirable* was that the proclivities of a bad nature should be curbed and re-directed, that future responsibilities should be prepared for, and that certain social attitudes should be inculcated.

A further illustration of this same important point about the valuational basis of needs-statements is provided by a consideration of educational books which are imported from other cultures or societies significantly different from our own. For here one may find needs-statements the warrant for which is culture-relative, and which are therefore invalid when exported, in spite of all their research support. P. T. Young mentions 'the need to maintain one's status within one's group, the need to win pre-eminence, the need to save one's face, the need to avenge an affront . . .' (Young, 1943, 150), which nicely illustrate this point. In connection with cultural relativity, however, mention might be made of Maslow's useful distinction between 'basic' or 'deficit' needs and 'growth' needs (Maslow, 1955). 'Deficit' needs are those without which we become 'mentally ill', such as safety, love and respect, and which are therefore needed by anyone. Much more relative, however, both to cultures and to individuals within cultures, are 'growth' needs. By these Maslow means, for example, the need to be a good artist, carpenter or scientist. The notion of 'growth' used here will be further considered in the next chapter.

The second of the defects earlier mentioned related to the assumption that an education which starts from the 'needs of the child' will solve the problem of motivation. But the trouble here lies with the equation of what a person *needs* with what he *wants*, for the motivational problem is only in some degree solved when the relevant item comes to be wanted. From the judgement that '*x* needs *y*' it by no means follows that '*x* wants *y*'. John may need Latin to enter university though he loathes the subject. The patient may need to convalesce for a month though what he wants is to return to work immediately. And certainly such an optimistic conclusion was unwarranted in the elementary school, where it was not even expected that children would want what they were judged to need.

Child-centred theorists, however, are sometimes apt to take wanting as a *criterion* of needing. If a child in an infant classroom wants to play with sand, *ergo* he needs to. Sometimes perhaps indeed he does: if, for example, he would in that way work out some phantasy or emotional problem which it is desirable that he should work out. But even here, to say that he needs to play with the sand is to say more than simply that he wants to. It is to sanction his desire as being an urgent or important one that *ought* to be satisfied, and plainly not all wants come into that category. Taken as an unrestricted generalization, the statement that what children need is what they actually want would be as near as makes no difference to saying that we should start from children's *interests*. Such a shift in the argument is at least to be desired for giving up talk about a curriculum based on children's needs, for as Komisar has pointed out, every curriculum is a needs-curriculum (Komisar, 1961). No-one dreams of including in the curriculum anything that is not needed, and hence no criterion of choice is or could be furnished by resort to bare statements of

'need'. As has already been argued, the heart of the matter lies in
the prior notions of what is valuable or desirable. It is here that a
criterion of choice must be found.

INTERESTS

There is an immediate difficulty in attempting to determine by
an appeal to children's interests the values which are to furnish
the aims of education. The difficulty is that in one sense of
'interests' it would be a mere tautology to say that values are to
be determined by a consideration of interests, for 'my interests'
may mean 'my good'. In this sense, when we say that something
is 'in a person's interests', we mean that it is 'for his good'. The
opposite of 'interested' in this sense is not *un*interested but *dis*-
interested. A disinterested person in some connection is one whose
own good does not touch upon the object being considered, and
who therefore may be relied upon to show a measure of impartiality in any dispute over it. On the other hand, as A. R. White
points out, an *interested* party may be a bored one. Thus *this* sense
of interest, like the concept of need, always involves values, and
does not advance at all any inquiry into the values that are to serve
as aims in education. Over some of a child's interests there will be
complete agreement, as with his basic interests in health, safety,
security and some form of education. But when we ask precisely
what form of education is in a child's interests, dispute and dis-
agreements are very likely soon to break out.

An important dispute concerning interests, in this first sense
that we are now considering, is over who is to determine what a
child's interests are. Is he the best judge of this, or are the adults
who stand in some teaching relationship to him, whether that of
parent or schoolteacher? Few would say that a child is always the
best judge, quite without qualification, but if this is denied then
immediately we are faced with the possibility not only of his being
unaware what his real interests are, but also of his being incapable
of grasping what they are, even if they are explained to him.

Hence the problem of motivation and the uphill battle often presented by the task of educating someone. Indeed, it is arguable that the value of education is something which can be perceptible to us only in retrospect, since it is only because we have been educated that we are in a position even to judge what our real interests are.

Furthermore, if this is so one can see how, in a consumer-orientated society, education will necessarily seem unattractive by comparison with glamorous attempts to flatter and entice one's existing tastes and preferences. The problem is as old as Plato, who draws attention to it in such dialogues of his as the *Lysis*, *Gorgias* and the *Republic*. Even John Stuart Mill, whose essay *On Liberty* is a classic defence of the individual's right to determine for himself what is in his interests, excluded children from such liberty of choice. He said: 'It is, perhaps, hardly necessary to say that this doctrine is meant to apply only to human beings in the maturity of their faculties. We are not speaking of children . . .' (Mill, 1859, ch. 1). At the present stage of our own argument, however, we are not yet in a position to advance conclusions on this problem. It will be raised again in the next chapter.

The second sense of 'interest' is that in which we speak of a person as feeling interested as opposed to feeling *un*interested, or even bored, by something. Feeling interested, in this second, mentalistic sense, is not simply a matter of paying attention, since we may be obliged to attend, or do so merely out of politeness. Again, we can attend or not at will, and hence we can be told to attend and blamed for not doing so, but we cannot feel interested at will, or be told to feel interested and blamed for not being so. We can only contrive conditions which are favourable to arousing interest. We can, of course, be told to look interested, for what that is worth. Again, feeling interested is not a mood, sensation, or emotion, any of which could distract us from the object of our interest. It is attending and feeling positively inclined so to attend, whether to someone or to something or to our own activity. Such a positive inclination to attend may be transitory only, as with the mercurial interests of very young children, or it may be a more settled disposition, as with hobbies and other regular pursuits centred round some activity or object (see A. R. White, 1964, ch. 7).

There is, however, considerable implausibility in the suggestion that the aims of education are to be determined by considering the interests which children may actually be found to have at any given time. Why should interest in this sense be thought to be valuable, or even stable? Indeed, there is a formal logical fallacy, the 'naturalistic fallacy', in attempting to infer judgements of value from statements of empirical fact, such as the empirical fact that someone's inclinations are such-and-such. The invalidity of the inference becomes more obvious if one considers an interest in pornography, crime, or poking animals with pins, as possible premises of the supposed inference.

There was really no problem here for the elementary school tradition, since it was never expected that children would show much interest in what was thought good for them by their teachers. As William James put it in one of his Talks to Teachers:

It is certain that most schoolroom work, till it has become habitual and automatic, is repulsive, and cannot be done without voluntarily jerking back the attention to it every now and then. This is inevitable, let the teacher do what he will. The repulsive processes of verbal memorizing, of discovering steps of mathematical identity, and the like, must borrow their interest at first from purely external sources, mainly from the personal interests with which success in mastering them is associated, such as gaining of rank, avoiding punishment, not being beaten by a difficulty and the like. Without such borrowed interest, the child could not attend to them all. (Quoted by Knight, 1950, 238.)

Indeed, not only was it thought unlikely that children would be interested in much schoolwork, but there were also thought to be positive advantages in their not being so, since splendid moral opportunities for training both the will and character were thereby presented. As Sir John Adams put it: 'The good-old-grinders have on their side the undoubted fact that drudgery has to be

faced in this world, and it does not seem an unreasonable contention that our pupils should be made to face drudgery as soon
as possible' (Adams, 1928, 212).

School was to prepare one for 'life', and 'life' was drudgery.
Furthermore, the blame for a child's failure in school could, on
this view, be attributed to the child himself as a moral lapse on
his part. He was lazy, careless, did not try, did not attend, would
not concentrate, etc. And to try to remedy this situation by appeal-
ing to interests was 'soft pedagogy', a capitulation to the unredeemed inclinations of our nature. It was not surprising, therefore, that child-centred reformers should have countered this with
the assertion that children are by nature *good*: only environments
and formal teachers are bad. But the view that children are by
nature good, which is another doctrine shaped by opposition, is
one that we shall consider further in connection with the concept
of growth. For the moment it is more important to register something of the real force of this child-centred reaction.

Four important contentions in this reaction deserve serious
attention here, two of them programmatic and two justificatory.
First, it would be altogether better, it was said, if the learning of
basic skills were not simply a matter of isolated drills and exercises, but were achieved by harnessing such learning to actual
interests. Secondly, these actual interests could also provide starting points from which to move onward and outward in educationally valuable directions.

A third contention was that there are good psychological
reasons for adopting such procedures. Motivation would be
improved because action would be more meaningful. Individual
differences would not be ignored by the pursuit of uniform standards of attainment for all, so that slower learners could have
work adapted to their pace and faster learners need not be held
back. Learning would be more permanent and more integral to
the child's development, because gained under the pressures of
whole-hearted interest. Fourthly, it was said that to start from
existing interests in this way was the only method of teaching

compatible with respect for the child as an individual person having a distinctive point of view and distinctive purposes to pursue. Hence this was the only *moral* way of teaching children. But attractive as these counter arguments appear, they require some important qualifications, though not qualifications to be made in a spirit of grudging concession.

First of all, the child-centred programme of starting from children's interests ignores the fact that the direction of these interests is something which will have been socially learned, and hence the educational value of these interests will depend on the value of the influences which have been at work on a child outside the school. He may come from a social environment which is indifferent or even hostile to the values and purposes of the school. In such an environment, work and status may owe little or nothing to education. Even children coming from what is materially a more prosperous background may still be 'culturally underprivileged', thinking that the good life is one of indiscriminate television viewing in a bookless home, with aimless car drives as the main break in the routine. In such circumstances, simply to start from existing interests is to trivialize the curriculum and to give the school's endorsement to interests which may even be positively at variance with the purposes of education. Something more in the nature of an educational crusade would seem to be needed here, as indeed is recognized by the Plowden Report's recommendations concerning 'educational priority areas' (Plowden Report, ch. 5).

Secondly, this programme is too dominated by the polarities of either/or against which Dewey warned. It is simply false to assume that the choice lies between following actual interests and some kind of authoritarian brow-beating. Yet according to Nancy Catty, for example, we should consider children's 'likes and dislikes very carefully, for it is obvious that it is better to educate along the lines of children's interests than against them' (Catty, 1949, 4). But the teacher has an important function to perform in stimulating *new* interests, and in seeing that activity does not simply confine itself to an already gained repertoire of knowledge and skill. He may introduce a quite new topic, such as a practical study of aspects of the weather, but then reasonably expect fresh interests to develop in response to this initiative of his as the work progresses, so that its eventual outcome will never be entirely foreseeable at the start. Such a developing interaction of stimulated and then responsive interest defies the polarities of either/or. Nor should the teacher's position be forgotten as a prestige-bearing person in an institutional setting. In general, children are expectant of initiatives from teachers and ready to give new things a try. This is not at all to say that the initiative should always come from the teacher, or *always* from anybody. Such a view is simply doctrinaire, though child-centred theorists can be as doctrinaire about freedom for the child as any 'rigid formalist' can be about the opposite.

Thirdly, though interest as a motive is doubtless very desirable, it may reasonably be doubted whether everything of educational value ever could be learned under its steam alone. We may well reject the elementary tradition's views on training the will and preparing for 'life's drudgery', yet it remains the case that it will be an unusual classroom in which *all* use of artificial incentives can be wholly dispensed with, and in which *all* practice, and the development of good work habits, is gladly undertaken 'because it is seen to be meaningful'. Children, like everyone else, can plainly see the point of something, still find it a bore, and be grateful for any devices by means of which the teacher can enliven this part of the proceedings.

Yet the optimistic belief that everything can be done in a state of euphoria has never quite disappeared. As B. Z. Friedlander recently commented:

From statements such as those that increasingly occur in the literature on children's motivation the teacher is led to infer (*a*) that children almost uniformly have powerful cravings to learn; (*b*) that the teacher's real function is simply to get the pupils started in the right direction and then stand aside to avoid being trampled in the stampede to acquire knowledge; and (c) that if otherwise 'normal' children do not follow this pattern the teacher is doing something wrong. (Friedlander, 1965, 24.)

Nevertheless, the fact that an unbroken gradient of expanding interest, from childhood to the educated man, cannot be regarded as anything other than a chimaera is no justification for perpetuating dreary routines, mechanical exercises and drudgery generally, when classroom practitioners have demonstrated these to be unnecessary. And the child-centred reaction has been an important force in searching for and developing more interesting ways of teaching.

But, finally, we now have to face the fact that all of this has done nothing to advance our inquiry into the values which should determine the aims of primary education. As is often said, it is characteristic of child-centred theories to be 'strong on methods, weak on aims'. *Which* new interests is the teacher to stimulate, or selectively to encourage? *Which* basic skills are to be harnessed to existing interests? How far is one justified in identifying what children are interested in with what is in their interests, in the first and evaluative sense of 'interest'? A third child-centred concept which must now be examined in an attempt to answer these questions is the concept of 'growth'.

Chapter Three

AIMS (2): GROWTH

An absolutely central concept in the reaction against the elementary school tradition has been the concept of 'growth', yet in spite of its importance one searches in vain for an adequate and coherent elucidation of the concept. Rather, it functions as a symbolic image, pregnant with meaning and rich in emotional appeal. 'Let the end of the process of growth be what it may. Our business is to grow' (Holmes, 1911, 295). One thing, however, is very clear: children in the elementary tradition did not grow. Indeed, that tradition was 'the very negation of growth. *All* its characteristic features: the buildings, classrooms, classes, enforced attention, and notions of 'learning', were like a conspiracy to insulate children from everything that could help them to grow; and a conspiracy which for many was only too successful' (Isaacs, 1961, 36). The contrary image of the processes of education is, of course, that of 'moulding', or imposition from outside on plastic material, and in so far as growth is defined at all it is always opposed to such moulding. Indeed, this moulding may well be regarded, as it is in Gesell's writings, as being all one with fascism.

The notion of education as 'growth', and therefore as something to be set in the sharpest contrast to any kind of moulding, can be found in Rousseau's *Emile* (1762), in Froebel's *Education of Man* (1826), in Holmes's *What Is and What Might Be* (1911), in Dewey's *Democracy and Education* (1916) and *Experience and Education* (1938), and in the various volumes on child development written by Gesell and his collaborators, such as *Infant and Child in the Culture of Today* (1943) and *The Child from Five to Ten* (1946). Before one can even begin to determine one's own attitude to the growth ideology, however, it is necessary to try to unravel some of the many strands that are woven together in it. As will soon become clear, it marks a synthesis of many very different kinds of consideration.

MATURATION, CHILD DEVELOPMENT AND READINESS

(a) *Maturation*. Let us begin with what is, perhaps, the natural home of the notion of growth, namely the development of the biological organism. Furthermore, let us narrow this down to those aspects of organismic development which bear upon learning. We then have a fairly clear sense in which one might speak of the *maturational* factors in learning. Empirical evidence can be abundantly produced to show that it is a waste of time to try to teach babies to walk, climb, or use the potty before certain physical developments have occurred, more particularly developments in the cerebral cortex and in the nervous system generally, such as the myelination of the nerves. Such facts as these, to do with physical maturation, are regularly presented and interwoven with statements about educational growth, and they are, of course, true, interesting and important. But three qualifications to this must be added at once.

First, this evidence would seem to be much more important in considering the pre-school child than in considering schoolchildren. Even at five, the child's brain is already ninety per cent of its adult weight (Plowden Report, para. 21). Secondly, this evidence is negative in its practical bearings. It makes clear what you *cannot* do, not what you ought to do once conditions are present which make learning possible. To show a sequence in the emergence of various capacities in no way determines that those capacities should then be exercised and still less does it show on what in particular they should be exercised. For example, a great deal of evidence could be furnished on maturation in connection with learning to use one's toes, but that would not show either that the toes ought to be used, or for what they ought to be used. In fact, in our own culture such evidence would have no practical relevance at all, except perhaps for manually deformed or armless children whose only opportunity for tool-using lay in the feet.

Thirdly, a caution needs to be entered concerning the presentation of scientific evidence on maturation interwoven with statements about *educational* growth. It makes it look as if the very different kinds of statements being thus made also have the same solid, empirical basis. Educational recommendations then appear to be empirical necessities, rather than the ethical *choices* of particular individuals, groups, or cultures. For example, M. Pickard, in *The Activity of Children*, writes of maturation, readiness, and 'growing points', in a way which assimilates neurological conditions for walking and climbing to *eagerness* conditions for getting children to write letters, post them and take on responsibilities. (Pickard, 1965 passim, but especially pp. 25, 28 and 72.)

(*b*) *Child Development.* Closely connected with maturation is the notion of 'child development', though it merits separate examination. At first sight, 'child development' looks as if it would be a descriptive science with a rich observational basis. Statistical techniques would be applied to these observations to reduce them to a comprehensible account of how children actually do develop, both for good and ill, and in different social classes and societies. This science would thus be a kind of cultural anthropology, and in fact Gesell sometimes refers to his own work as indeed being such. He says, for example, 'the age norms are not set up as standards and are designed only for orientation and interpretive purposes (Gesell, 1943, 2). Many of the findings of such a descriptive science would of course be culture-relative: true, for instance, only of the Arapesh, or of the Polynesians, or (as in Gesell's case) of middle-class Americans. Moreover, such a science could perfectly well be developed for what most of us would regard as an evil society, such as a Nazi one. Age norms might then show when Jews are first spat at, when negroes are first kicked, how the growing boy forms a concept of the *führer*, or when he joins various party organizations, etc.

But in fact child development is not just a descriptive science. It does include a great many true observations, but these are selected and marshalled to show us a certain *chosen ideal* of personal growth. The observations are presented as *guidance*. 'Generally the guidance will be implied in the statement of the traits and will not call for detailed formulation' (Gesell, 1946, 70). But it is there, and there very strongly. 'Developmentalism is the *very opposite of fascism*, for it *acknowledges the individuality* of the child and wisely concedes that all his behaviour is subject to the natural laws of human growth' (Gesell, 1946, 452, my italics). Again, 'the concept of growth has much in common *with the ideology of democracy*', and the details of growth are presented 'with special reference to the factors of maturity which *must determine our whole outlook* upon the nature and needs of the individual child' (Gesell, 1943, x, my italics). If we want the point made explicitly, and without intrusive italics, then: 'this philosophy of child development and of child guidance assumes a democratic type of culture' (Gesell, 1943, 57).

Child development, at least of Gesell's kind, is therefore not an ethically disinterested science at all but a system of normative guidance for achieving a particular chosen ideal of 'maturity', as that term is concretely understood by middle class Americans. It is indeed a 'technology', as Gesell says (1946, 39). This means that the logical structure of such child development studies is as follows: (i) there is a particular chosen ideal, by no means shared by everybody but taken for granted as being the obviously right one (which of course it may indeed be, though this is never argued); (ii) there is a set of selected but probably true observations which are presented in such a way as to give guidance on how to achieve the chosen ideal.

Whether we do or do not agree with the chosen ideal which is the central organizing principle, however, it is clear that a 'science' of child development which goes beyond cultural anthropology, and therefore cultural relativity, ceases simply to be science and becomes a sustained attempt at ethical persuasion, rich in favoured recommendations. One result of this is a chronic unclarity as to the *grounds* on which this or that is being argued. Another result is that the recipients of the advice are never quite sure whether what is required of them is attention to the latest findings of empirical research, or some kind of personal ideological conversion. The truth, of course, is that both are required.

(*c*) *Readiness*. A central doctrine of the growth ideology in education has been that the teacher's task is assiduously to observe the child in order to detect signs of maturing 'growing points', best indicated perhaps by spontaneous, felt interests. It is admitted, however, that the detective work involved in this is far from easy, for 'we are still far from knowing how best to identify in an individual child the first flicker of a new intellectual or emotional awareness, the first readiness to embrace new sets of concepts or to enter into new relations' (Plowden Report, para. 9). On this view, pupil and teacher are like plant and gardener, and the school is a child-garden, or kindergarten. Teachers 'must regard themselves as gardeners watching development, ready to feed the growth, ready to prune, restrain or weed according to need; trying to help each child to grow to the best he may be; not worried to make all the plants the same, but trying to bring about that they shall grow, so that the whole garden shall be a harmony' (Priestman, 1952, 127).

The educational method embodied in these recommendations and sentiments can, accurately enough for our present purpose, be set out in three main propositions. First, the teacher ought to provide a 'stimulating environment'. He must neither force the growth as if in a hothouse, nor must he miss its latest unfoldings, but he may stimulate and he must observe closely. What must he observe? The answer is given by the second proposition: the teacher ought to observe signs of 'readiness'. He must watch for the maturation points, the growing points, in order not to miss his cue. But once he has been cued by the unfolding and appearance of an interest in the stimulating environment, then what is he to do? Third proposition: the teacher ought to feed and guide the further growth of the interest, though in what direction he ought to guide it is typically left unsaid.

But which is 'the environment', and how do we know what is 'stimulating'? Is it the physical environment, the social environment, the environment opened up by books, or what? And are there not a host of valuations concealed in the apparently biological notion of 'stimulation'? On what grounds is this rather than that *chosen* by the teacher as being 'stimulating'? The problematic notion of 'environment' is one that will be taken up again later, in the chapter on experience. For the moment, the important point to fix on is that choices and valuations as to what ought to be offered as 'stimulation' are being taken for granted, left unexamined, and presented as somehow being quasi-biological dictates.

Furthermore, an important ambiguity in the terms 'maturation' and 'readiness' is being introduced. The appearance of interests is being presented as the same sort of thing as the maturation of the nervous system. Just as you cannot teach bladder control before certain physiological developments have occurred, so also, it is assumed, you cannot teach mathematics before the appearance of an appropriate interest. But this is a disguised prescription. You *can* teach before the appearance of an interest. What is really being urged is that you *ought not* to, so that it is not a matter of maturation at all but of value-judgements. The ambiguity concerning 'readiness' is therefore now seen to be between (i) 'not ready' because you could not succeed even if you tried, and (ii) 'not ready' because, in the light of various value-judgements left unstated, it would be undesirable to try yet, though in fact you could try and could have some sort of success. The classic illustration of these confusions is, of course, 'readiness' in connection with starting to read, taking 'reading' here to mean grasping the appropriate meaning of a text on the basis of continuous word-recognition.

We can, indeed, distinguish at least three kinds of readiness here. First there is the physiological necessity of maturation of the eyes and relevant nerves. Secondly, there is the conceptual necessity of understanding something of language before any responses made to print could properly be called 'reading'. Both of these requirements could be, and sometimes are, met by the age of three. This must clearly be so since children of three and even younger do in fact learn to read if they are intelligently taught (see the three articles on 'Reading Readiness' in *Educational Research*, vol. IV, no. 1, November, 1963). Indeed, in the view of R. Lynn, 'with the disposal of the spurious concept of delayed perceptual maturation it seems doubtful whether the concept of reading readiness has sufficient substance to be worth retaining' (Lynn, loc. cit., 14). Thirdly, there is the growth theorist's requirement for readiness that some interest in learning to read should appear, an event which he expects to occur at various ages from five to as late as eight or so.

Of course, he does not just wait passively for this interest to appear, as did Rousseau, who saw no need for reading before twelve or thereabouts, but he stimulates it, for example by putting out attractive books and by reading interesting stories out of them. It is worth noting, however, that the growth theorist may disallow an interest in reading, even if it does appear before the expected age. This may be disallowed on the grounds that the 'laws of growth' require that a child must play at that 'stage'. Note the grudging tone of concession in this passage:

It is a good plan to provide some sort of reading material as soon as the children come to school. So many of them come in a mood of keen expectation. They think that they are going to learn to read and write and do sums, and it can be a real disappointment to them if they are made to engage in what they call 'play' all day. So, for those children who want it, and perhaps are ready for it, let us provide some simple reading material. (Goddard, 1958, 31.)

But really, we see, they ought to be playing.

When we are presented with views about 'readiness' then, it is worth asking at least these four questions: (i) Readiness for what exactly? (ii) Are the conditions of readiness necessary, as are physiological and conceptual conditions, or only in your view desirable? (iii) In either case, can these conditions themselves be actively brought about, or must we wait for some inner ripening to take place according to the 'laws of growth'? (iv) If the conditions are not necessary but only in your view desirable, what are the values by which your views on desirability are taken to be warranted and

how do you justify them? Thus the complexity of the growth
ideology, and the heterogeneous nature of the considerations
that it runs together, begin to emerge. This, however, is only a
start.

ESSENTIAL NATURES AND NATURAL GOODNESS

The next strands to be unravelled are those to do with the child's
'essential nature', the notion of there being 'laws of growth' in the
unfolding of this essential nature, and the notion of the child's
'natural goodness'. These ideas have historically been at the centre
of the Froebelian doctrine of growth. They are to be found also in
the writings of Gesell, who was greatly influenced by Stanley Hall's
view that the individual's development recapitulates the cultural
history of the race.

The idea of the child's 'essential nature' is that of some kind of
pattern for perfection which is held to be present in embryo in the
child and which will reveal itself in a developmental unfolding if
only the environment and external stimulation are right. The
model is obviously a biological one. Froebel writes of the appointed
time at which the duckling takes to the water, the chick scratches
and the flower blooms, while Gesell explicitly likens the development of mind to the growth of plants. Edmond Holmes provided
a succinct statement of the idea when he said: 'The perfect manhood which is present in embryo in the new-born infant, just as
the oak-tree is present in embryo in the acorn, will struggle un-
ceasingly to evolve itself' (Holmes, 1911, 241).

The process of unfolding is one which is taken to have definite
stages, much as the development of frogs or butterflies has definite
stages, and each of these stages is taken to have its characteristic
perfection. This has an interesting implication in that it follows
from it that children are to be seen not as imperfect adults so much
as perfect children. 'Nature would have them children before they
are men . . . Childhood has its own ways of seeing, thinking, and
feeling; nothing is more foolish than to try and substitute our ways'

(Rousseau, 1762, bk. 2). Admittedly, Emile at twelve may *seem* to be just a rough, vulgar little boy, but really he has unfolded 'the perfection of childhood'.

Froebel was most anxious to revise ideas about play, and tried to do this by exhibiting play as the perfection of the kindergarten 'stage': 'Play is the highest phase of child-development—of human development at this period; for *it is self-active representation of the inner—representation of the inner from inner necessity and impulse*' (Froebel, 1826, para. 30, his italics). It can easily be seen that the doctrine of 'natural goodness' is already implicit here, both in the references to 'perfection' and in the assumption that what is 'natural' in the unfolding is right. 'Let us lay it down as an incontrovertible rule that the first impulses of nature are always right; there is no original sin in the human heart' (Rousseau, 1762, bk. 2).

Perhaps the first and most obvious objection to this kind of thinking is to point out that it ignores the *social* in human development. The growth of a person is something which necessarily takes place in a social group, and in this respect is quite unlike the unfolding of plants. To try to strip away the social influences that have been at work in the growth of a person, and in the formation of his self-concept, is not to get back to some core of being which is the essential person, but to be left with crude and undifferentiated basic desires and appetites. It would, therefore, be a gross underestimation of the influence of the social to see it as an inessential accretion, or a merely facilitating condition, in the growth of persons. Even individualism is a particular social tradition, with a social history, and not at all a stepping outside of society.

Some growth theorists, for example Dewey, give full and explicit recognition to the role of the social. Others, such as Holmes, take account of it by culling the best of some thousands of years of social history, and then projecting it, as it were, into the new-born child and asserting it to be at work there as the sympathetic, aesthetic and scientific 'instincts'. Gesell constantly vacillates between talking of natural laws which 'can be comprehended only through science and yet more science' (Gesell, 1946, 452) and on the other hand stressing the role of culture, particularly American middle-class culture.

The second objection is an epistemological one. How do growth theorists *know* the 'laws of growth', or what 'optimum development' is? They make it look as if one only had to *observe* growth in order to find this out, but that cannot be right. To start with, psychoanalysis has drawn our attention to the hate, jealousy, rivalry, aggression and destructiveness to be found, even in the youngest children, alongside of love, sympathy, kindness and gentleness. Neither assertion of the goodness nor assertion of the badness of original human impulses would therefore seem to contain the whole truth. In view of these undesirable impulses, it would indeed seem, as Nathan Isaacs says, that 'the one picture which we can no longer retain is that of the infant whose life is all happiness and goodness and content and who has only to be spared gratuitous mistakes or mishandlings to grow from bliss into untroubled and joyous and more and more nearly divine perfection. The Froebelian vision of the child is a dream' (Isaacs, 1952, 212).

The epistemological objection may be put in another more fundamental way. It is a formal logical fallacy, the 'naturalistic' fallacy again, to try to infer judgements of value from empirical facts, such as the fact that some organism is actually developing in such-and-such a direction. The admission of this may be forced in the following way. Plainly not *all* actual development is good. No growth theorist is going to admit that Hitler 'grew', in the lauded, ideological sense of 'grew'. They speak of deviance, blocking, stunting and distortion. Then *by what criterion* is deviance from 'proper' development identified? The answer to that will be the statement of what the growth theorist regards as valuable, and the ruling out of deviants will show both that his values cannot be simply inferred from what actually happens and that his 'laws' are not entirely natural ones.

When so pressed, however, the vagueness and the unexamined nature of the values involved may become apparent. 'The ideal self is, in brief, perfect Manhood. What perfect Manhood may be, we need not pause to inquire' (Holmes, 1911, 290). But this is sheer evasion. Furthermore, if one does pause to inquire, it sometimes turns out that the 'essential nature' of the child is not an *individual* nature, all his own, but a universal nature, common to all. This is so in Holmes, as also in Matthew Arnold's earlier *Culture and Anarchy*, though not in Froebel. We learn from Holmes that 'Growth is, in its essence, a movement towards that perfect type which is the real self of each individual in turn, and the approach to which involves the gradual surrender of individuality, and the gradual escape from the ordinary self' (op. cit., 206).

If this is the view of our 'essential nature', authoritarianism returns with a vengeance, albeit under the cloak of a solicitous interest in the child. Now we hear of having to be 'forced to be free' (Rousseau), we learn that 'indoctrination has an important role' (Gesell, 1946, 38) and we find that children who do not want to make creative models out of cornflake packets, or who do not want to do whatever 'wholesome growth' requires, are regarded as having nasty little wills resistant to the loving teacher's beneficent ministrations. Alternatively, they may be regarded as being pitiable in some way. Nor is this result surprising when one realizes that the growth ideology developed out of late-eighteenth- and nineteenth-century Romanticism, a nest from which both Marxism and fascism emerged as two of its broods.

Another common characteristic of these ideologies, further to the 'real self' doctrine, is a belief in the inevitable march of *processes*, with individual choice, decision and agency having little or no place. In Marxism this appears as a belief in historical determinism, with the individual capable of no more than assisting in the birth pangs of history. In the growth ideology it appears as a sense of being caught up in biological processes of ripening and unfolding. 'The total ground plan is beyond your control. It is too complex and mysterious to be altogether entrusted to human hands. So nature takes over most of the task, and simply invites your assistance' (Gesell, 1964, 6). And Gesell's guidance on how to assist should be accepted because everything 'is now changing under the irrepressible tide of cultural forces', and 'participation rather than detachment is the trend' (op. cit., 38). Of course, a pervasive feature in Gesell's work is his affirmation of the uniqueness of the individual, yet for all that a sharp sense of people as individuals is precisely what one misses in his 'pageants', 'vistas' and 'sweeps of development'.

A private life about which others do not know or in which they do not share is suspect on any such view. 'It would lead us far astray if we considered the psyche to be an occult force, which operates behind the scenes' (Gesell, 1946, 19), while private ideals always have for Dewey 'something rotten' about them. There should be just one organically developing public process in which individuality finds a place only as a distinctive configuration of manifest behaviour patterns, or as having something distinctive to contribute to the group. (For some sustained criticism of the absorption of individuals into historical or 'democratic' processes, see J. P. Sartre, *The Problem of Method*, or D. Riesman, *The Lonely Crowd*.)

But it would be very unfair to see such tendencies in every version of the growth ideology. These disturbing features do not accompany a belief in individual, rather than common and public, 'essential natures'. Abraham Maslow's work on growth motivation is a good example of this more individualistic strand. In his view, 'growth' begins when all basic or 'deficit' needs have been satisfied, so that the individual can occupy himself with the constructive work of 'self-actualization'. Self-actualizers like privacy, detachment, meditativeness and independence. They can see people and things as they are, undistorted by their unfulfilled needs. Growth is still a matter of 'laws' but they are 'the laws of their inner nature', and growth itself is defined 'as the various processes which bring the person towards ultimate self-actualization'(Maslow, 1955).This is a doctrine with a philosophical history going back to Spinoza and earlier still to Aristotle. Moreover, Maslow has an unusual and refreshing awareness that it is not just experimental data that he is presenting, but an *ethic*, albeit a vague and unargued one (see Peters, 1958, ch. 5 sect. 2).

This self-consciousness about having a distinctive *ethical* position in 'treating' people is still more apparent in P. Halmos's *The Faith of the Counsellors*. Halmos comments on the psychotherapist or social caseworker that 'while he unprepossessedly labours to help his clients he cannot but communicate to us some fairly definite propositions about his work and about the nature of man, and these propositions do not seem to follow from his scientific assumptions' (Halmos, 1965, 4). As a statement of aims, however, the growth theory as so far discussed is disappointing. We are still no nearer to knowing what the aims of primary education ought to be. The Froebelian goal of complete unfoldedness, as Dewey rightly says, 'represents a vague sentimental aspiration rather than anything which can be intelligently grasped and stated' (Dewey, 1916, ch. 5 sect. 2; see also Peters, 1964a, sect. 2).

Let us finally turn, therefore, to the more systematic attempt to get a criterion of value out of 'growth' which was made by Dewey himself. Many of the philosophers and educational theorists who have attempted to produce arguments here, have not, of course, always used the *word* 'growth'. Variants on the same idea are 'self-development', 'well-rounded, many-sided, balanced and harmonious development', 'full development of potentialities', 'self-realization', 'self-actualization', 'maturity' and 'positive health'. But Dewey actually does say that the aim of education is growth, or rather, that education *is* growth.

DEWEY ON GROWTH

An account strikingly similar to Dewey's, in its formal features at least, was given by the English philosopher, F. H. Bradley, in explaining what he meant by 'self-realization' (Bradley, 1927, Essay 2). Bradley observed, as indeed must be observed in any evaluative account of growth and its variants, that not everything a person might do can count as self-realization. What, then, are the criteria of value in terms of which the self to be realized is to be picked out? They are two, both apparent, Bradley said, if we reflect upon our purposive strivings and our implicit pursuit of some ideal of happiness. First, the self to be realized must be an integrated unity, in which there is no pursuit of disconnected ends but a coherent pattern or style of activity, with one thing linked to another as means to ends. Secondly, the self to be realized must not be an impoverished one achieved by the curtailment of desires or by withdrawal from activities, but must be a self of some richness, in fact, the widest and most inclusive self that we can harmoniously achieve.

Bradley conceded that we may sometimes wander a bit from our main path, and occasionally be inconsistent, but he thought that in every person's activity there is implicit some ideal of happiness, some self he is trying to realize. Now these two criteria, which for brevity we may call integration and richness, are almost exactly the same as the criteria which Dewey proposed as definitive of educative growth. This is not really surprising, since both Bradley and Dewey owed much to a common source, namely the work of the German Idealist philosopher Hegel (1770–1831), who was also a contemporary of Froebel.

(a) *Dewey's theory*. Dewey's discussion of growth is scattered throughout his educational writings, but is principally to be found in *Democracy and Education*, chapters four and five, and in *Experience and Education*, chapter three. If we try to put his discussion together into a brief statement, it might be expressed somewhat as follows. Nothing is of value to us unless it can enter into our experience in a way which enables us to realize what is valuable in it. An education which looks only to the future, and which sees no value in present experience except as a preparation for that future, is therefore not something which a child can be expected to embrace. Moreover, since he will see no value in what he is now required to do, it will not even succeed in the purpose of preparation, but will remain something isolated in his mind and thoroughly disliked. It will engender, as a collateral learning, attitudes of resistance which alienate him from any desire to go on learning once the pressures of imposition from outside are released.

The general statement, that nothing is of value to us unless it can enter into our experience in a way which enables us to realize what is valuable in it, therefore applies as much to children as to anybody else, though Dewey does not say, of course, that what children find valuable in learning must be precisely what *we* know to be valuable in it. He is only saying that they must see *some* value in it. For Dewey, growth is the enjoying and further development of experiences realized by us to be valuable, and hence the aim of education is to bring about such a growth.

But can nothing else be said about the experiences that are valuable? Surely the educator must know this if he is to have any useful role to play? To answer these questions, Dewey furnishes us with two criteria which, as has already been pointed out, are very similar to Bradley's. They are the criteria of interaction and of continuity. There is 'interaction' in a situation to the degree that I am engaged by it, and hence do not have to deal with it as an intrusion, disconnected from my real concerns and attended to only by a reluctant effort of will. To be so engaged *is* to find something of value in the experience. To the intrinsic value of the experience itself, 'continuity' adds an instrumental value, one which the teacher will often be more aware of than the child, and indeed one which it is an important part of the teacher's task to secure. Sympathetic understanding will enable the teacher to appreciate what his children find valuable: only his maturity and greater experience will enable him to secure the instrumental value of continuity.

By 'continuity', Dewey means that an experience should be of such a character that it is fruitful for later experience, in opening up still more and richer possibilities of experience, and in giving greater control over it. Acquiring mechanical habits and memorizing boring information are not fruitful in this way. Nothing is later enhanced thereby. At best the present performance will later be capable of replication. There will be no expansion of curiosity, no

widening of horizons or increase in sensitivity. With this, contrast
learning to talk or to read: whole new environments are opened up.
A valuable experience, then, is one which has the two features of
interaction and of continuity.

There is much that is both attractive and persuasive in this
account of growth. Who would not be attracted by such a picture
of integrated purposes, richness and open-ended expansion? But
it may be questioned whether anything more than formal value-
criteria can be established in this way. It may be asked whether the
persuasiveness of the account does not derive from Dewey's tacit
assumption that *we all know* what a 'mature' teacher would be,
capable of securing the 'right' continuities in present interactions
and hence of wisely seeing that they are 'fruitful'. If one does have
such suspicions, the only way to confirm or remove them is to test
out Dewey's proposed criteria against counter-examples deliberately devised to refute them. Only if they stand up to such testing
may we have any justified confidence in them.

(*b*) *Value and desire.* But first of all, the relation of value to desire
deserves some comment. For what is most valuable in human life
cannot simply be equated with what is actually desired by particular
people at particular ages. We may perversely desire what we know
to be harmful. We may desire things of little or no consequence.
Much more importantly, we may desire what we *mistakenly* regard
as being the most worthwhile that there is. It is important to notice
here that the question is often very much one of things being more
or less valuable, rather than of their being either valuable or of no
value at all. The idea that all of a person's desires might be for
things which were in no way at all *regarded by him* as valuable is
indeed a perverse one, if not entirely unintelligible, for what could
such a person's notion of a 'reason for action' be? (Melden, 1961,
ch. 12.)

The next point calling for comment is Dewey's contention that
nothing is of value unless it enters into our experience in a way
which enables us to realize what is valuable in it. But this is only

an epistemological condition: nothing can be *realized* to be valuable by us unless we can experience, or at least readily imagine, what it is about it that makes it valuable. This is quite different from saying that nothing can *be* valuable for us unless we realize it to be so. For what we can experience or imagine is subject to all sorts of contingent limitations, such as not having been educated in the appropriate way.

People often walk round art galleries or listen to orchestral concerts, but remain mystified as to what is valuable here. Nor is this surprising, for the perception of aesthetic value calls for a particular kind of education, not just good will together with the appropriate sense organs. It is a pardonable exaggeration to say that the whole problem of education is to bring people to an appreciation of values which, at present, they cannot fully understand. This is why it was suggested in the previous chapter that the value of education is something that one can properly appreciate only in retrospect. It is therefore important to distinguish between something's *being* valuable, and its being *known* to be valuable, for something may be valuable though we do not, or at least do not yet, realize it to be so. It even makes sense to talk of there being valuable things of which *nobody* yet knows, though there may be little point in doing so.

The epistemological condition for the making of value-judgements does, however, raise three important problems. First, if I have to experience, or at least to imagine, what it is that makes something valuable before I am entitled to assert its value, then what actual value-judgements I am in a position to make will depend on who *I* am. And we are not all the same in what we experience or can imagine. I may see what is valuable in boxing, but not in biology, while you may be absorbed by the carbon cycle but totally at a loss to see the merits of so-and-so's footwork. This painting I have done may be treasured by me but regarded as totally uninteresting by you. That is the first problem, and one which makes the discussion of what is worthwhile in human life both fascinating and interminable.

Secondly, this epistemological dependence on who *I* am nevertheless does not set fixed limits to the range of what I can appreciate, for I can always change. This immediately destroys any simple-minded picture we might entertain of observing children's 'natures' and then arranging appropriate activities to match them. To do this is one of the errors of 'starting from the child', namely the error of accepting his existing nature as a datum to which we can only accommodate. Hence the Existentialists' constant reiteration that our nature is not a given, but is itself always in question. 'Who am I?' is answered as much by choice and decision as by discovery, and hence no-one can settle the problem of what to regard as valuable as if it were a theoretical problem which already had a definite solution, if only one could find out what it was. Our nature is always to some extent in question (Sartre, 1943, passim).

Finally, there is the educator's special problem of his right to make value-judgements as to what is good *for others*, which presupposes the objectivity of his value-judgements. This problem is made more acute by the familiar fact that the others will often not be in a position to appreciate what he, the educator, is trying to disclose, even if an objective justification can be given for regarding it as valuable.

To summarize, then, Dewey's theory of value calls for the following comments. We may be mistaken in what we regard as desirable. There may be very worthwhile activities and pursuits of which any individual is at present quite ignorant. To say that something is desirable or worthwhile, or valuable, is a bolder claim than simply to say that one now wants it. Yet Dewey would seem to be right that we have no *reason* to regard anything as desirable unless we can experience, or at least can readily imagine, what it is about it that makes it desirable, whether it be mountaineering, studying history, carpentry or playing the violin. But thirdly, this does not warrant jumping to the conclusion that our range of appreciation is limited by our nature, for our nature is not fixed, like a dog's or a sheep's, but can itself be put in question and is at least to some degree alterable by education.

Finally, there is the problem of the *educator's* reasons for regard-ing something as valuable. Here it is difficult at first to see how one can substantially advance much beyond Mill's position when he argued that to appreciate that *x* is better than *y*, and how it is better, one must have experience of both. Perhaps this ought to be weakened a little by saying that one must experience or at least be able readily to imagine both. To try to be more precise than this would be difficult without being more specific as to what one was comparing. But one thing is clear: a parent or teacher will generally be in a much better position to make sound value-judgements than will a child. Furthermore, he will generally be able to see a value in many things of which a child has as yet little or no inkling.

(*c*) *Morality and desire.* An important further objection to Dewey's theory still remains to be made. If interaction and continuity are supposed to be sufficient conditions for claiming something to be valuable, what are we to make of the growing egoist, criminal, or tyrant? Is not the fact that their ambitions and activities expand and grow just the trouble with them? Bradley was to the last locked in struggle with what he called 'the bad self', the one that was not to be realized, and Dewey himself was far from unaware of the problem. In *Experience and Education* he considered the case of the burglar, the gangster, and the corrupt politician. Tacitly, he con-ceded them 'interaction', but thought that he could rule out their activities with his criterion of 'continuity', for such occupations restrict, rather than enlarge, further experience: or so Dewey said.

To this we may object, in the first place, that it would seem to be an empirical claim, and by no means an obviously true one, that a criminal's experience is impoverished in this way. What of the things his access of wealth purchases? What of the risk, excitement, and constant exercise of intelligence involved in judging collabora-tors and evading detection? Is Dewey doing more than indignantly insisting that the unjust *must* be unhappy?

In the second place, on Dewey's account it looks as if the activi-ties of a tyrant would be ruled out only if they were unsuccessful, so that only the fact that one could not get away with tyranny would make it wrong. This is not morality, but simple expediency. In fact, Dewey's theory of value would seem to share a general defect of all growth theories in that rich and integrated selves can be realized which nevertheless are morally evil.

Dewey, of course, is not recommending moral evil to us; he is just taking morality for granted and assuming that it, like everything else of value, can be comfortably housed under his two roofing criteria of interaction and continuity. If one examines his views more closely, one finds that morality is actually being smuggled into the interaction criterion, much as Holmes smuggled it in as an instinct. 'Interactive' situations, it appears, are situations in which we learn to *accommodate and adapt* to others, in which adult interventions are *fair*, in which satisfactions are *made widely accessible*, and so on (*Experience and Education*, chs. 3 and 4).

But once 'situations' are defined in this morally evaluative way, what is Dewey's warrant for equating them with the actual situations in which individuals busily do their growing? What has happened to Bradley's 'bad self'? Definition is a gratifyingly simple way of making everybody moral, but it does leave over the practical problem that behaving morally is something that has to be learned. It involves giving up some urgent desires out of consideration for the desires of others, and it puts us under obligations we are not always delighted to fulfil. Neither of these two things would seem to be spurts of 'growth', unless that too is now redefined to include morality. But in that case, why not openly talk about moral values in the first place?

GROWTH AND PERSONS

It is not the purpose of the present chapter to argue that there is nothing true or valuable to be found in the growth ideology. Its purpose is in fact a threefold one: first to try to disentangle the many different kinds of consideration which are being run together in the notion of growth; secondly to show where this conflation involves confusion and concealed persuasion; and thirdly, to try to extract such elements of truth and value as must surely be contained in such a powerful synthesis. Before proceeding to the third of these purposes, however, it may be useful to draw together some of the more important points that have so far been disentangled.

Perhaps six main points have so far emerged, as follows: (i) There are true observations to be made concerning maturational sequence in the emergence of various human capacities. These observations, however, are negative in their practical bearings, being of the general form 'you cannot teach a child x until y has happened'. But whether you ought to teach x anyway, and what particular x it ought to be, are necessarily left undetermined. (ii) Beyond these observations to do with maturational sequences, talk about 'laws of growth' is confusing. It ignores the very variable social influences and hence areas of possible choice, which enter into any child's development, and moreover which importantly determine in which direction his development is to go. This confusion is facilitated by the quasi-biological notion of a 'stimulating environment', which again conceals the fact that choices and preferences are involved.

Again: (iii) 'Readiness' conflates maturational, conceptual and evaluative conditions by presenting them all together as a single empirical necessity which leaves us no choice at all. Really, however, we do have a number of possible choices, a preference for any one of which needs some justification. (iv) 'Child development' is not just a disinterested science descriptive of how children in different classes and societies actually do develop but, at least in Gesell, takes for granted a particular ideal and cites various probably true but selected observations as guidance in achieving that favoured ideal. A recipient of the findings of child development is therefore in part being invited to assent to certain empirical facts and in part being persuaded to adopt a specially favoured outlook on children and what they ought to become.

Further: (v) The growth ideology is constantly involved in a fallacious presentation of its guiding values as somehow arising out of processes, and hence as being quasi-biological dictates. The

fallacy may be that of supposing observation of the *actual* course
of growth to show how it *ought* to go, or it may be that of simply
equating in meaning what is actually wanted, or now felt to be
interesting, with what is really desirable or really needed. Sometimes, of course, the same thing will answer to both descriptions,
but not always, and the wedge can be forced by asking for the
criterion for ruling out some things as 'stunting growth', or some
felt interests as being undesirable. (vi) Finally, a general criticism
is that natural processes of growth and unfolding are confused with
social processes of teaching and learning. Yet if one goes back
to some of the major philosophers who first talked in terms of
development, such as Hegel and earlier still Aristotle, it is the
social that one finds being stressed, and indeed even overstressed.

Is there anything of ethical value embedded in the growth ideology which, when extracted, is seen to be acceptable? Our own
suggestion is that there certainly is, and that it might well be called
the ideal of a personal autonomy based on reason. There are two
aspects to such an autonomy, the first of which is negative. This is
independence of authorities, both of those who would dictate or
prescribe what I am to believe and of those who would arbitrarily
direct me in what I am to do. The complementary positive aspect
is, first, that of testing the truth of things for myself, whether by
experience or by a critical estimate of the testimony of others, and
secondly, that of deliberating, forming intentions and choosing
what I shall do according to a scale of values which I can myself
appreciate. Both understanding and choice, or thought and action,
are therefore to be independent of authority and based instead on
reason. This is the ideal.

At least two arguments can briefly be presented as a justification
for accepting this as a basic or minimal ideal. First, even for me to
question whether I ought to test my beliefs and make my choices
according to my own reasoned judgement, rather than in obedience
to authorities, is already to have decided in favour of autonomy;
for I am asking for *reasons* as to what I ought to do, and taking it
for granted that it is *I* who will decide the merits of the answers.

Secondly, such an ideal of personal autonomy based on reason is to be more positively sought and valued on four chief grounds: (i) that through it we can achieve integrity and thus not be involved in self-deception, or the deception of others; (ii) that it permits us to develop an intelligible and well-grounded knowledge of our true situation in the world; (iii) that it permits and encourages us, in that situation, to pursue the good as we ourselves judge it, though correspondingly it makes us personally responsible for our choices; (iv) that consistency with its own principles already requires that we be fair in our dealings with others. Its central values are, therefore, independence, reason, integrity, truth, freedom of individual choice and judgement concerning what is worthwhile, responsibility, and fairness. It may be regarded as certain that sometimes some of these values will be in conflict with others, but that is a painful fact which every human ideal unfortunately has to face.

A question may be raised at this point as to the further justification of these values, for unless they are justified further are they not simply arbitrary commitments? The reply to this is as follows. First of all, no-one could *understand* what was meant by independence, integrity, freedom of choice and so on without also seeing that each of them had features such as could well make it highly prized. Therefore anyone who does understand and value these things must at least be allowed to have good reason for doing so. Of course, this is not sufficient to make such valuation entirely non-arbitrary, for there might conceivably be other things more highly to be prized. However, such valuation is rational if these three conditions are satisfied: (i) that there is reason to value these things (which is seen as soon as it is understood what they are); (ii) that such valuation is always open to criticism (which is not being denied); (iii) that the valuation survives such criticism (the onus now being on others to show other things to be more valuable).

In short, 'rationality' is being understood here in terms of always being open to criticism, rather than in terms of having an ultimate justification. It is not being taken, as some sceptics have taken it, to require that everything that logically could be questioned should be so, a requirement which can be satisfied by nothing short of logical invulnerability. Any ideal that is more than formal is always vulnerable to criticism, but only a craving for certainty which itself ought to be questioned could lead one to say that an ideal vulnerable to criticism was therefore no more than an arbitrary 'commitment'. Rationality lies in holding all one's beliefs open to criticism, not in having a logically watertight justification for them all. Indeed, the demand that everything be justified is self-refuting, since this demand is itself unjustified and therefore counsels its own rejection. But everything can consistently be held open to criticism, though one cannot, of course, criticize everything at once (see Bartley, 1964, chs. 4 and 5).

Faced with serious criticism, the basic ideal described above might require some further justification. Certainly more could be said about the interconnection of the various values mentioned. But to engage in such further exposition and justification here would take a disproportionate amount of space and would mean a very lengthy digression. For the time being, then, it will be taken for granted as a basic ideal compatible with various conceptions of happiness. In the light of it, some of the notions examined in this and the previous chapter can now be given a reasonably clear meaning. 'Needs of the child' now get some specification and backing, and a defensible notion of what is in his interests can be formed. 'Growth' is seen to be towards a chosen human ideal and not a mindless quasi-biological process. Furthermore, such an ideal will be rich in the procedural guidance which it gives in teaching and, together with certain other assumptions yet to be explained, it will also be of central importance in curriculum construction.

In conclusion, it might be worth indicating how the valuable core of the growth ideology that has been extracted here should so readily have been confused with quasi-biological notions of growth, and of the unfolding and flowering of inner potentialities. There are two main points of analogy between the human ideal and the natural process which invite the conflation. First, the ideal is opposed to any kind of authoritarian dictation or imposition, whether by parties, priests or public pressures. Analogously, growth is from within and is to be contrasted with moulding from without.

Secondly, the ideal is one of increase in understanding, gaining in independence, and progressively coming to realize what is involved in forming intentions, making considered choices and accepting responsibility for them. It thus has a definite direction, even though particular ends have to be chosen that are not already given or fixed. Analogously, the causal processes of unfolding growth can be seen teleologically as being directed towards some end, such as the flowering of the plant or the emergence of the butterfly. Thus both involve continuity and movement in a definite direction, though in the one case there is self-direction and in the other only a biological process.

Analogies, however, are not identities, and sufficient confusions have come to light in the course of this critical appraisal of the growth ideology to invite the question whether this notion, when taken as a model of the educational situation, may not have outlived its usefulness. Certainly it will be of no value in the next step of our inquiry into aims, for that involves an attempt to construct a curriculum conformable to the ideal that has already been outlined. Where is the content of such a curriculum to be found? Certainly not in the scrutiny of plants, nor even in a search for some hypothetical 'nature of the child'. Fortunately, we are saved from the truly unenviable position of having to make unguided and wholly innovating choices here by the fact of living in a society with a funded historical experience concerning what is worthwhile. Indeed, to recognize as an ideal a personal autonomy based on reason, to support it, and to devise agencies and institutions to cultivate it, is itself something belonging to a particular social tradition, and one which is not found in every society by any means. In fact, so far as the majority of people are concerned, it is something confined to liberal democracies alone.

Chapter Four

AIMS (3): A CURRICULUM

Out of its five hundred and fifty-five pages on primary education, the Plowden Report devotes three and a half to the discussion of aims. A substantial part of even that tiny portion is devoted to doubts, not quite about whether it is actually worth *having* any aims, but about whether there is any point in trying to state them. 'General statements of aims,' the Report says, 'tend to be little more than expressions of benevolent aspiration which may provide a rough guide to the general climate of a school, but which may have a rather tenuous relationship to the educational practices that actually go on there' (para. 497).

Now this depressing verdict may well be true of *some* statements of aim. It would be true, for example, if such statements were made in terms of growth and its variants. Indeed it is just such vague phrases that the Committee did have in mind, which is a happy confirmation of the arguments directed against such talk in the previous two chapters. Small wonder that the Committee were depressed if 'phrases such as "whole personality", "happy atmosphere", "full and satisfying life", "full development of powers" . . . occurred again and again' (para. 497).

What, then, would a good statement of aims look like? From the depressing verdict quoted above, one might infer that it would be an accurate general statement of what the schools *actually do*, for such would be a better guide, and less tenuously related, to 'the educational practices that actually go on there'. But that is to leave everything as it is: the habits, conventions, traditions, confusions, uncertainties and practices which have outlived their usefulness, and simply to describe it with a few abstractions. This would probably put a pleasing enough decorative finish on a well established tradition. As Dewey says: 'The traditional school could get along without any consistently developed philosophy of education. About all it required in that line was a set of abstract words like culture, discipline, our great cultural heritage, etc., actual guidance being derived not from them but from custom and established routines' (Dewey, 1938, ch. 2). Yet if there is one thing that is true about primary education today, it is that there is no such clearly established tradition to carry on. It was the burden of our introductory chapter to show this and explain why it is so. Reflection upon aims was never more needed than now, with the remains of the elementary tradition in rapid eclipse and no end of often contrary advice being offered as to what to do next.

A good statement of aims, then, is badly needed, but cannot simply be a description of what actually already goes on. Nor, as the Plowden Report rightly indicates, should it consist of the vaguer phrases of child-centred theory. Nevertheless, it is the very nature of statements of aim to be general. That is not a fault, but precisely their function, for the purpose of getting clear about aims is to provide an overall orientation and direction for some complex activity, such as educating may be taken to be. It is not the function of a statement of aims to settle the details of organization and methods, but to state the most general objectives which these are to subserve.

Because of their generality and the difficulty of formulating them even with such precision as generality permits, aims often remain only implicit in a practice. The spur to making them explicit is, first of all, a measure of disorientation and confusion, such as we now have, and secondly, the need to formulate them for explanation to new entrants to teaching. In spite of the difficulty of the task, then, there ought to be much to be gained at this time from any sustained attempt to clarify our aims and examine their validity. To do this is surely at least part of the task of the philosophy of education.

The Plowden Report is a work of recommendation and therefore logically cannot avoid implying views as to what is educationally valuable. If it has failed to state the aims which guide its major recommendations, or cannot see much value in trying to do so, then it will not have escaped having them. They will simply lie implicit only and therefore unexamined, scattered through the body of its recommendations. For example, in chapter two, one hundred and eighty pages away from the chapter on aims and embedded in a mass of empirical research, there lurks this statement: 'At the heart of the educational process lies the child. No advances in policy, no acquisitions of new equipment have their desired effect unless they are in harmony with the nature of the child, unless they are fundamentally acceptable to him' (para. 9).

This is sheer assertion and not the hard empirical fact it appears to be. It is, in fact, a familiar child-centred doctrine: (i) 'the child has a nature', which is a dubious metaphysical assertion; (ii) 'we ought to adopt the principle of always starting from and being acceptable to that nature', which is an unargued ethical recommendation. Is this 'nature' an individual or a universal one? Is a person's 'nature' supposed to be some fixed given thing which can be discovered and to which one can only accommodate? Ought one to start from it, whatever 'it' should be, quite unconditionally? What are these assertions doing embedded in empirical research anyway?

Thus, in leaving the question of aims unexamined, a whole series of important questions is begged. The implicit structure of the evasion is this: (i) leave alone any attempt thoroughly to discuss the aims you have in mind; (ii) at a more concrete level, enter into discourse which can in fact be engaged in only if your aims are already tacitly presupposed; (iii) then everyone will be so absorbed in the detail as not to notice the overall direction in which you are going.

However, to do it justice, the Plowden Report does not completely fail to give any explicit statement of aims, though what it does give is meagre and unsystematized. Put in the terms of our own discussion, it is implicitly advocating personal autonomy. This is so in its reference to discovery, being creative, and 'being one-

self'. As to the other values of which we are still in search, the
Plowden Report gives a hint and a caution. The hint is that our
children will live in a society which will require them to be adaptable workers and discriminating consumers, and which will provide
them with leisure to fill and others to live with. The caution is the
usual child-centred one 'that knowledge does not fall into neatly
separate compartments' (para. 505). But perhaps we need not take
this caution too seriously, since the Report itself then proceeds to a
discussion of the curriculum which is divided into eleven separate
and conventional subject compartments (ch. 17).

Then ought our own inquiry to turn at this point to a discussion
of subjects? Traditionally, of course, the curriculum has generally
been thought of in terms of subjects, though just what 'subjects'
are, and upon what principle they are to be identified and demar-
cated, are questions rarely raised. The obscurity of the principle of
division is readily seen in the various fragmentations which English
undergoes: spelling, handwriting, composition, comprehension,
dictation, poetry, drama, oral composition, story-time and so on.
Professor Dottrens, in an international comparative study, identifies
three hundred and fifty-two 'different' subjects taught in primary
schools in various countries (Dottrens, 1962, 91).

Even if a more rational basis of division is sought by referring
to the various disciplines which are distinguished and pursued in
different university departments, many problems still remain. The
aptly called 'explosion in knowledge' has multiplied and fragmented
these disciplines beyond any possible hope of democratically repre-
senting them all even in the secondary school curriculum, quite
apart from that of the primary school. If some attempt at representation were made, obviously no more than a tiny portion of each
discipline could be included. By what criteria would such a portion
be selected? Would it be simplicity, logical priority, motivational
appeal, social utility, examinability? And if that were settled, would
the result not be a compartmentalization which was arbitrary from
every point of view except that of the convenience of university
teaching and of research? In view of these difficulties, to launch

PPE—E

straight into a discussion of 'subjects' would obviously be premature, and possibly also misconceived.

RELIGION AND VALUES

A fresh start might be made on the problem of the values which are to give content to the curriculum by noticing a feature of the concept of education itself. 'Education', in its most unrestricted sense, means the process by which people are brought to an understanding and appreciation of what is valuable in human life. Such processes are not, of course, confined to formal schooling but importantly take place in the family and other out-of-school associations, in fact wherever there is a concern for the disclosure of what is valuable. 'Education' is, therefore, itself an evaluative concept, though a formal one which leaves the value-content undetermined. Only in an ironic sense do we refer to influences which change people for the worse as 'educational' (Peters, 1966, ch. 1).

In our own society in the past, a major value-orientation has, of course, been given by religion, which has presented a systematic set of beliefs about God, man and the world, together with various prescriptions as to the way of life thought consequent upon those beliefs. Formal education, therefore, was orientated by religious doctrines. As the Plowden Report points out, the elementary school itself partly derived from the National Society for the Education of the Poorer Classes in the Principles of the Established Church, which was founded in 1811 (Plowden Report, para. 493). Our own introductory chapter sought to show how the theory of human nature accompanying those principles influenced the general ethos of the elementary school tradition. This influence of religion on primary education is one that has remained, more particularly in the legal compulsion to hold some form of communal school worship, in the holding of classroom prayers, in the giving of religious instruction, and in the convention of always placing religion first in official recommendations regarding the curriculum, as in the Plowden Report.

Nevertheless, the status of religion in schools is becoming increasingly problematic as the meaning and truth of religious doctrines come to be questioned, inside the churches as well as among those who have dissociated themselves from anything to do with religion. Whether contemporary theology will be able to reconstruct from this a set of doctrines which is both intelligible and convincing remains for the future to show, though there are many who would argue that the attempt at such a reconstruction must be misconceived. (See some of the articles in Flew and MacIntyre, 1955). Some of the views presented by modern theologians are certainly attractive, but on the other hand it is often hard to see why they should be thought to be religious, at least in any sense of that word which implies God, the divinity of Christ and immortality. This problem of meaning and truth in religion is one which we shall take up again later.

One thing, however, is very clear. It is indisputable that the doctrines of religion have been brought into serious question by many who have gone to the trouble to reflect on them carefully and critically, and whose views are therefore worth rather more than are those of people who, on this matter at least, are no more than the echoing repositories of what they have been told to believe in childhood. And if, as is indisputable, the truth of the doctrines of religion is seriously doubted, on excellent grounds, then it is an objectionable form of indoctrination to propagate these doctrines in common, public schools as if they were unquestionably true. One might also add that it would be equally unjustified to refer to them as if they were unquestionably false.

It may be argued that 'indoctrination' is, essentially, not so much a matter of doctrines and of doubts about their truth, as of getting people to believe things in such a way that nothing, not even good counter arguments, will shake those beliefs (J. P. White, 1967, 181). This may well be so, but if it is so, then it is very natural that 'indoctrination' should have its main application in teaching such beliefs as those of religion. It is especially here that groups of people have an interest in establishing beliefs which will then be held with a conviction which the doubts and open disbelief of others will not shake. 'Catching them young' will obviously be a highly expedient policy for the indoctrinator. Nor, it may be added, is there any substance in the reply sometimes made to this that *everybody* indoctrinates, even the mathematics teacher. For first, whatever other sorts of teaching are *called*, important differences from the teaching of religion remain, and secondly, it does not in any case meet a charge to plead that someone else is up to the same thing.

This is not, of course, any objection at all to teaching *about* religion, which need imply only a belief on one's own part that certain things are the beliefs of others. This could be done by an atheist without any loss of intellectual integrity, just as a religious person could teach about Marxism. Moreover, there are good cultural and historical grounds for teaching *about* religion. But the schools do more than this. 'Many teachers openly admit that they attempt to attach their pupils to some worshipping community' (Cox, 1966, 61). But prayer and worship are hollow, meaningless activities unless certain beliefs are held about the object to which they are addressed, namely God. One cannot pray or worship *about* religion; such activities are logically impossible apart from the presupposition of an actual belief in God. The external forms of prayer and worship can, of course, be compelled, and recalcitrant children can, individually or collectively, rebel with a 'prayer strike', or be punished for not praying, as sometimes happens in secondary schools, but this could be regarded as valuable only by one who esteemed cynicism a virtue.

The objectionable character of religious indoctrination, which derives from inducing conviction in the truth of beliefs which are in fact highly questionable, has certain further consequences. First, it puts an aspect of education in a liberal democracy exactly on the same footing as a corresponding aspect of education in totalitarian states, and hence removes the ground of objection to these totalitarian practices. Yet the attempt to deform the growth of rationality by appropriating an area of belief for the indoctrinator is as objectionable when the indoctrination is religious as when it is political. For example, one cannot view without misgivings a situation which leads Plowden to recommend that the 'teacher should not try to conceal from his pupils the fact that others take a different view' (Plowden Report, para. 572).

Secondly, religious indoctrination is incompatible with respect for personal autonomy, in that it positively encourages dependence on authority for what one is to believe. It is a characteristic but shameless inconsistency on the part of some child-centred theorists that they encourage questioning, testing truth for oneself, and critical acceptance of beliefs in all fields except that of religion. Here they capitulate, and even gladly, to authoritarianism. Thus children 'should not be confused by being taught to doubt before faith is established' (Plowden Report, para. 572). But if they do ask questions, how should one reply? 'They should be given an honest answer' (loc. cit.). What are the actual alternatives that render this particular recommendation necessary?

A third possible consequence of indoctrination, and of its violation of autonomy by 'getting faith established first', is that it runs the risk of unfortunate collapse should those in whom faith has been so established later come to doubt. The subsequent collapse would be highly unfortunate, in the first place because of the general distress attendant on such a disorientation, with its sense that 'everything has become meaningless', and in the second place because morality will have been bound up with the now disavowed beliefs. The indoctrinator cannot dissociate himself from some responsibility for this state of affairs. In part, at least, he has himself been the cause of this distress, a reflection which ought to give him pause in his view of himself as a distributor of unqualified benefits.

The consequences for the teachers themselves are hardly less disagreeable, since the present unsatisfactory arrangements breed frustration, hypocrisy, timidity and a loss of intellectual integrity. Teachers who dislike giving religious instruction, or leading prayer and worship, are presented with unfair choices. In the classroom, they have to choose between either doing something that they detest, or loading colleagues with extra work and causing a general disturbance of arrangements. In respect of their legitimate ambitions, teachers lacking religious convictions must in practice choose between furtive concealment of this fact and an honesty that may well block promotion (see Plowden Report, 491, section 4, and para. 563).

Before blaming those who choose furtive concealment, one should look at the unjust institutional pressures which make this a condition of their advancement, just as when children are cheating a great deal one should look at the classroom régime as well as at the individual child's morals. Finally, a teacher who lacks religious conviction but who does achieve a headship must then either exercise his ingenuity in evading the legal requirements for the daily act of worship, or succumb to all sorts of rationalization in order to preserve his self-respect.

An apparent counter to these arguments for ceasing to indoctrinate or initiate into religious practices, and so do no more than teach *about* religion, is provided in the Plowden Report. It cites some opinion surveys which show there still to be a majority of teachers and public in favour of religious teaching, though only about one-fifth of them are also in favour of their own active church membership. But the Plowden Report's reasoning here looks less like reliance on a principle of argument than picking up a handy stick which has a certain usefulness. For elsewhere in the Report, in connection with corporal punishment, the *same* conditions hold (in fact, absolutely overwhelming and convinced majorities in this case) but the *contrary* conclusion is drawn, namely to go counter to majority opinion and lead the way to change. 'We believe . . . that the primary schools, as in so much else, should lead public opinion, rather than follow it' (Plowden Report, para. 750).

But if there is one thing that a principle of argument will not allow, it is having the conclusion whichever way it currently happens to suit. Unfortunately, one cannot, as D. J. O'Connor justly observes, 'claim the benefits of reason without acknowledging its risks' (O'Connor, 1957, 125). Our own view is that the primary schools should, for the epistemological and moral reasons already given, lead the way on religion, for which a sufficient legal change at the present juncture would probably be that what is at present an obligation be reduced to permission.

Questions of what is true and right are never settled by an appeal to the fact of a majority opinion. That is to appeal to who says so rather than to what makes it so. This is not to deny that determining what is true and right is often very difficult, and that it may sometimes be preferable to abide by the majority's wishes rather than run the dangers of riding roughshod over those with whom one disagrees. Even those whose views one takes to be unconsidered or in error are still persons, and hence deserving of respect. But since the present discussion is an attempt to change opinion by argument, and not an actual political attempt to change practice by coercive legislative acts, it stands in no need of respecting existing majority wishes but can simply urge what seem to be highly relevant considerations in this matter. The indoctrination of religious beliefs and the initiation of children into religious practices will therefore be assumed to be no proper part of the primary school curriculum. It will also be assumed that they ought to be separated from such proper devices for getting institutional cohesion as the school assembly.

VALUES AND THE CURRICULUM

The position at which we therefore arrive is this. Our society presents not just one monolithic world-view, but many, often competing, views as to what is valuable in human life. And in respect of this plurality of values a common, public school, which in practice the great majority of children are legally compelled to attend, ought not to be in any way partisan as between these varied ideals of life, even if some of them have the backing of powerfully entrenched interests. There are other educational agencies which will present partisan views to those who choose to listen to them. With what values, then, can the school be concerned in its educational function? Out of what is it to construct its curriculum? There are, it would seem, two valid and, in part, overlapping answers to these questions.

First, in spite of the modern pluralism on values, there remains a substantial content to the notion of a person's good on which there is rightly a consensus of opinion, and from which some indications for procedure and content can be gained. These considerations are, in part at least, hinted at in Plowden's remarks on the features of the society into which children will grow up. They include: (i) being economically viable, which points to the 'basic skills', and to mathematics, science and language; (ii) living with others in a justly ordered form of social life, which points to social science and moral education; (iii) engaging in worthwhile leisure activities, which points to a rich range of extra-curricular provision, such as field games, clubs and societies, both religious and secular; (iv) enjoying physical and mental health, which points to physical education and to an informed sensitivity in teacher–pupil relationships and classroom arrangements; (v) appreciating the value of the forms of personal relationship involved in love, family life and friendship, which perhaps indicates such things as sex education, 'domestic science', and moral education once again.

The second answer is less obvious but extremely fruitful. It derives from the basic ideal outlined at the end of the previous chapter. If the school is not to prejudge the choice of the values by which one is to live, this does not mean that it has no role at all in relation to that choice, for rational choice is itself rich in its presuppositions. First, and most importantly, it presupposes that one will indeed choose, and not just be told what to believe and do. To presuppose that is already to take for granted the value of personal autonomy, which was discussed at the end of the last chapter. This, as was pointed out, has many implications for the procedures of teaching.

But the exercise of rational choice also presupposes, as the other aspect of a personal autonomy based on reason, a well grounded understanding of one's situation in the world. This leads on to the fundamental question: what forms of understanding are basic constitutive elements in rational choice? The answer to this would seem to be as follows: mathematical, scientific, historical, aesthetic and ethical. But before tracing further the possible curricular implications of those basic elements in rational choice, four points demand careful clarification: (i) What is meant here by a 'form of understanding'? (ii) What is the principle upon which the various forms are distinguished? (iii) In what sense are they 'basic' elements in choice? (iv) How do they relate to the emotions?

Forms of understanding. First of all, a distinction must be made between having an understanding of something and just possessing some information about it, though the one necessarily involves the other, of course. A fairly widespread view of knowledge, especially in the elementary school tradition, is of it as an assemblage of isolated facts memorized in more or less the same verbal form in which they were learned. This might appropriately be called the 'rucksack' view of knowledge, for the two relevant features of a rucksack are that it is loosely attached behind and that it can be more or less full. The rucksack view of knowledge, then, equates it with useful information, and since only its usefulness is what makes it worth having, the grounds for regarding it as true are really not very important. It is sufficient if one has it on good authority, such as that of a teacher. All of this fits in very well with the general authoritarian ethos of the elementary tradition.

When the 1931 Report implicitly devalued 'knowledge to be acquired and facts to be stored', it was surely with such a rucksack view of knowledge in mind, as it has been with the many child-centred theorists since who have scornfully referred to 'subjects', and to the artificialities of setting up 'watertight compartments' between them. Of course, it is not asserted that knowledge has *no* value, which would involve an immediate and obvious paradox since this is itself something claimed to be known, but rather knowledge is implied to be no great thing by comparison with the joys of self-directed activity. Acquiring knowledge is therefore depreciatingly referred to as a process of 'topping up pots', 'plastering on facts' and 'verbalism', and its result is said to be one-sided people whose poor virtues can be revealed only in quiz programmes and examinations.

Furthermore, self-directed children can always get information when they want it because, first, they have good attitudes towards knowledge, even though they do not actually possess it, and secondly, they have learned how to learn, and have only to deploy this universal information-getting skill as the need arises to become as well placed as the next person. This skill roughly comprises a knowledge of the usefulness of reference books and of their classification, together with a certain facility in scanning indexes and tables of contents.

Neither the informational view of knowledge nor the child-centred reaction against it, however, begins to approach the kind of understanding intended in this book. Some would not even accord the title of 'knowledge' to such an assemblage of facts. Professor Scheffler, for example, writes that 'knowledge requires something more than the receipt and acceptance of true information. It requires that the student earn the right to his assurance of the truth of the information in question. New *information*, in short, can be intelligently conveyed by statements; new *knowledge* cannot' (Scheffler, 1967, 106).

Yet the confusion between the two things that Scheffler is carefully distinguishing occurs just because both *are* referred to as 'knowledge' in ordinary usage, and having something on good authority, such as that of a teacher, is regarded as giving the right to an assurance of truth. Admittedly, there must come a break with authority at some point: the teachers get it from the lecturers, the lecturers get it from their books, the books draw on the journals, and the journals, at least, were written by people who actually did some first-hand finding out. But of the investigators the children would know nothing, and would not need to in order properly to be said to 'know' what they had been taught.

If, however, we regard Scheffler as not just reporting to us about ordinary usage, but as recommending to us how knowledge should be regarded compatibly with placing a high value on personal autonomy, then his recommendation is very acceptable. If we value personal autonomy, then it is indeed fitting that a person should not simply think what others authoritatively tell him to think. He should either find out for himself, or at least be educated sufficiently to regard authorities as provisional only, and to form some estimate of the reasonableness of what he is told. For told he must be about many things.

Neither the rucksack view of knowledge as a loosely attached load of information, nor the gratifyingly simple idea that it is sufficient to have good attitudes and a universally applicable information-getting skill, meets the requirement of finding out for oneself, or at least forming a reasonable estimate of what one is told. The rucksack view emphasizes and encourages dependence on authority, while the 'good attitudes' view has a naïvely oversimple notion of how much can be learned simply by opening one's eyes or reading the words in a book. Understanding, in our sense, involves mental structures, ways of experiencing, which are progressively acquired only over a period and through the teaching of one who himself has such an understanding.

There are two elements constitutive of such structures: (a) systems of interconnected concepts and organizing principles, and (b) validation procedures for determining the truth, rightness or adequacy of the various ideas entertained. As soon as one inquires further into such an understanding, it turns out not to be a single, monolithic whole, but to involve quite distinct and non-arbitrary forms. Knowledge, in this sense, is not a seamless robe, but rather a coat of many colours. Far from being 'divorced from life', it slowly transforms our very notions of ourselves, of 'life' and of 'the world'.

The elucidation of these as yet somewhat cryptic hints will have to await our discussion of experience in chapter six, but two examples will meanwhile serve to illustrate the point at the primary school level. In the elementary school tradition, 'arithmetic' was regarded as a set of 'number bonds' to be memorized, and a set of computational procedures in which to be drilled. One learned one's tables and how to 'do' long multiplication: 'first, put down a nought, then . . .'. Nature study, to take a second example, consisted largely of learning the names of the parts, and facts about the lives, of various plants and animals talked of or read about.

In terms of structures of understanding, however, one would think rather in terms of number concepts and the basic laws of arithmetic, with procedures learned and practised within the context of coming to grasp such concepts and principles. The hope of this would be a greater degree of mastery shown both in better retention and in much wider transfer and application. And instead of a mainly classificatory and typically second-hand study of nature, there would be actual observation and an introduction of experiment. Plants would be grown, variables tested and measurements taken. Again, such an approach involves at least beginning to grasp concepts and principles which are far from being restricted to the actual cases observed.

The division of forms. The second point for clarification concerned the principle upon which the various forms of understanding are distinguished. Knowledge can, of course, be categorized in a great variety of ways (see Phenix, 1964, ch. 2), but our own categorization follows Hirst's (1965) in being based on distinct kinds of meaning and validation procedures, or alternatively, the sorts of concepts involved and the kinds of reason-giving appropriate. By 'reason' here is not meant the causal explanation of why someone comes to hold a particular belief, but the justificatory considerations which can logically be given for holding the belief. Each of the forms of understanding thus distinguished has its own way of answering the two questions 'what do you mean?' and 'how do you know?' And each has its own kind of 'critical thinking', and its own ways of being creative.

What actual forms of understanding men have evolved answering to this description can be determined only by an examination of the knowledge that we do now have, and not in any high-handed *a priori* way. Five such forms were mentioned above, with the primary school in mind, and we shall now proceed to a discussion of each of them. Nothing more than a brief delineation can be attempted here, but even a more elaborate attempt to state fully what each of them involves would necessarily leave out the unstatable, 'tacit' understanding of those who, from long experience, have come to know their way about in each of these forms of understanding (see Polanyi, 1958). One final caution: we are *not* at this stage concerned with how or in what order to introduce primary school children to these forms of understanding, but *only* with showing the distinctive nature of each of them.

(*a*) *Mathematics.* Mathematics has its own distinctive concepts, such as number, square root, prime, fraction, integral and function, though some of these *words* may have other uses elsewhere, of course. It also has its own validation procedure, namely a step-by-step demonstration of the necessity of what is to be established. Often there are many procedures to choose from. To demonstrate that $23 \times 12 = 276$, one might begin $23 \times 12 = (23 \times 2) \times 6$, or $= 23 \times (10 + 2)$, and so on, depending on such considerations as economy and elegance.

The validation procedures of mathematics are never empirical, never based on observation of the world or on experiment, but are demonstrations internal to the system specified by the appropriate set of axioms and definitions. If $6 + 4 = 10$, this is not because experience has shown it to be so, though exceptions might yet be found to occur. If six things and four things resulted in twelve things, that would not falsify the numerical equation $6 + 4 = 10$. It would only show that we *must* have made a mistake. Perhaps the groups of things were not counted correctly, or some things were counted twice, or the things were unstable. It is therefore highly misleading as to the nature of mathematics to regard it as an 'environmental study', as does *Primary Education in Scotland* (1965, ch. 20). This, however, does not imply that the *learning* of mathematics must begin with its logically most primitive elements.

In order to get application to the world, the non-empirical systems of mathematics require all sorts of auxiliary conventions to be adopted and assumptions to be made. Suppose it is asked whether there are more things in classroom A than in classroom B. Even this simple enough application of number concepts requires a convention as to what is to count as a 'thing': separate pieces of furniture? bodies? specks of chalk? molecules? Again, in the application of geometry to the world, conventions have to be adopted as to what in the real world will be taken to represent a 'point' (a pencil dot?), or a 'line' (the edge of a ruler?), or a 'plane' (a desk top?). If there is to be measurement, there must not only be an appropriate concept of the dimension of measurement, whether length, time-lapse, angle, weight, volume, speed or area, but a convention must be adopted as to what will count as a convenient unit of that dimension.

Assumptions also have to be made, fortunately usually quite safely, about the stability of the world throughout the period of our application of some mathematics to it. If things constantly divided or coalesced, like raindrops on a window, or if shapes bent and twisted all the time, the application of mathematics in such cases would become difficult or impossible. Indeed, the actual proclivity of the world to show such instabilities is something that has deliberately to be compensated for at the levels of accuracy at which a draughtsman may work, both in respect of his paper and his slide-rule. Neither keeps quite still (see Gasking, 1953).

(b) *Science*. The sciences, like the systems of mathematics, have their own interconnected concepts, though again words used to mark them may have other uses elsewhere. Such concepts include atom, magnetic field, cell, neurone, reflex, sublimation, trade-cycle, extended family, *anomie* and reinforcement. The validation procedure for a scientific hypothesis, put highly schematically, is to deduce what consequences one would expect upon such a hypothesis, and then to observe whether things are so. Instruments may be used to assist this observation, and experiment to control it.

If things are indeed so, that does not strictly 'prove' the hypothesis, for such an observation might also be the consequence of some *other* hypothesis. But if things turn out not to be so, then this does disprove some at least among the assumptions being made. With highly abstract theories, the step from theory to observation may be long and elaborate, even involving different classes of scientific worker, but there must be some point at which the theory stands or falls by actual observations.

Much of scientific reasoning is, of course, mathematical in form, but this does not mean that science is just a kind of mathematics. It only uses mathematics. Suppose I wish to predict the actual velocity of a falling stone after a given time. I may start from the equation $s = ut + 16t^2$, then differentiate to get $ds/dt = u + 32t$, and finally substitute given values for the variables, so finding that, starting from rest, the stone will be moving at 96 ft/sec after 3 seconds. But now there are two independent questions to ask: (i) Is the mathematics correct? (ii) Is what these inferences lead one to expect actually confirmed by observation? If the expectation is not confirmed, then no matter how impeccable the mathematics, the originally assumed law is false, or else its application in this case involves some false assumption. Observation, not mathematical accuracy, is the test of truth in science.

Scientific discovery does not typically begin with observation, however. If one tried to begin with observations, which observations should be made? Should one just take a notebook, look around and make notes? Should a psychologist just put some rats in a maze and then watch to 'see what happens'? What would be relevant? What would be worth observing? There is a popular view that scientific discovery is an accident that might happen to anybody. Did not Newton just chance to be in the orchard when the apple fell? Perhaps he did, but if so the point is that it was Newton who chanced to be there, and he was not just any observer but one who was preoccupied with certain problems, moreover problems perceptible only to people initiated into a certain tradition of inquiry. As Bruner remarks, 'discovery, like surprise, favours the well prepared mind' (Bruner, 1965, 607).

Science is not the progeny of a thoroughly promiscuous union between sense and the world, but is the outcome of an evolving tradition of inquiry. As such inquiry develops, the testing of a theory may well become no simple matter, since observational testing itself embodies theories, for example optical, physiological and psychological theories, but such difficulties largely lie beyond the primary stage of schooling. Even at that stage, however, the most elementary testing of one's expectations may go awry. 'Brass' may turn out to be magnetic (brass-coated steel drawing-pins), or a steel can may turn out not to be an electrical conductor (because it is painted).

(c) *History*. In turning from mathematics and science, the paradigm examples of standard validation procedures and therefore of 'objectivity', to history, art and ethics, the delineation of what is involved is much less clear-cut. It is therefore very tempting to be depreciative of these kinds of understanding, to accuse them of not providing 'hard facts', of having no 'laws' and hence, by implication, of being veritable carnivals of 'subjectivity'. But why should everything be judged by the standards appropriate to mathematics and science? It would be apposite here to recall Aristotle's caution when he said, in the first book of his *Nichomachean Ethics*, that it is a mark of an educated man that in every subject he looks for only so much precision as its nature permits.

History is not just the study of the past, for geology, palaeontology and the pre-history of man are also concerned with the past. History, roughly, is an attempt to construct, on the basis of such evidences as survive, a narrative of particular human actions and activities. It is not a species of imperfect sociology concerned with forming general laws about certain kinds of occurrence, such as revolutions, so much as with the happenings involved in some particular occurrence, such as the French revolution (Dray, 1957, ch. 2).

Since it is the actions and activities of men that are being described, the assumption is made that men do, for the most part, act rationally, if not always reasonably, so that the ordinary concepts of human motivation rather than specially constructed theoretical concepts give much of the meaning to the narrative. For example, when a historian of art tells us that in much of Northern Europe in the sixteenth century painters increasingly turned to the painting of portraits, as did Holbein, and when he explains this change as an effect of the Reformation, with its puritanical hostility to images as idolatry, then we readily begin to understand the motivation at work. Painters who had derived much of their income from painting altar-pieces and devotional pictures were now forced to seek a livelihood elsewhere, as in something unobjectionable like painting portraits of the well-to-do (Gombrich, 1966, ch. 18). We do not need a special *new* set of concepts to understand this; familiar ones will do quite well. But 'sixteenth century', 'Reformation' and even 'puritanical' may be regarded as distinctively historical concepts here.

Again, the validation procedures for historical narrative cannot easily be set out for all to see, and still less to apply. We might be tempted into a comparison with observation in science by pointing to such 'hard facts' as monumental inscriptions, coins, documents, buildings, utensils, books, weapons and so on. But the 'hardness' attaches only to what we have *now*; to see what these things *were* calls for interpretation, both as to their significance and their authenticity. 'The facts' have actually to be established; they are not just given for all to see (Walsh, 1951, ch. 1).

The establishment of 'the facts' is a process inseparable from the construction of the narrative. 'The historian validates evidence, constructs factual material and develops his interpretation, all at the same time, checking each aspect by reference to the others' (Perry, 1966, 42). Doubtless in the construction of such a narrative there are endless opportunities for bias and prejudice to operate, and doubtless they do operate, but the activity of being an historian is not a solitary one. His labour can be judged and criticized by his fellow historians, and his theses qualified, modified, or even shown to be quite implausible. Such assurance of objectivity as is possible resides as much in this public assessment and criticism as in the scruples of the individual, as Sir Karl Popper has so often stressed in connection with science (Popper, 1962, vol. 2, ch. 23).

(*d*) *The arts.* The aesthetic is not, of course, confined to the arts. We may be aesthetically aware of natural objects, such as the sea and the sky, and aesthetic considerations enter, though as properly subordinate to other considerations, into mathematics, science, history and every kind of practical activity, whether it involves the production of new or the arrangement of existing objects. Nor is the aesthetic confined to the beautiful, unless we so extend the meaning of that vague word until it does no work at all. A tragedy such as King Lear, or Rembrandt's portrait of himself as an old man, may powerfully impress us in many ways, but beauty does not seem to be one of them.

To confine our discussion to the arts, however, we can see clearly enough how the two features of concept and validation procedure enter into aesthetic understanding and judgement. The arts may, like history, use quite familiar words, such as rhythm, harmony, expression and balance, though giving them new senses or new ranges of application. New concepts may be evolved appropriate to composition and style, such as sonata-form, coda, foreshortening, flying buttress, Baroque, arabesque and atonality. New kinds of aesthetic object and new methods of production may be conceived, such as the concerto, the novel, the sonnet, fresco and etching. The arts, then, involve both familiar concepts in new applications, and quite new concepts arising in the development of different traditions and their criticism.

The validation procedures of aesthetic judgement present considerable difficulty to anyone seeking to state them, partly because there is no obvious sense in which the work of art is an attempt to approximate to something already 'given'. There appears to be no reality about which the work of art is an attempt to state the truth, as in science and history. In mathematics, once the definitions and axioms are laid down, the rest of the system, as yet untraced, is already by implication 'given'. In science and history, there is an attempt to find laws and furnish narratives which in some sense 'correspond' to what actually occurs or has occurred; otherwise they would be fictions and fantasies adrift from reality.

But a work of art is not already implied, waiting only to be traced, or 'there', waiting to be discovered. It is the artist's creation and, in a sense, its own world. Again, it would be very odd to respond to a painting or a piece of music by saying that one did not believe it. Even the most 'representational' of art, such as *trompe l'oeil* or the 'theatre of fact', cannot simply imitate without ceasing to be art. Art, even representational art, involves selection and rejection, rearrangement, accentuation, enhancement and omission (see Stolnitz, 1960, ch. 5). Add to this the disputed nature of many aesthetic judgements, and we may conclude that one man's opinion is as good as another's. We may see the picture or hear the music and find nothing at all to interest us in it, wondering if aesthetic judgement is not some kind of conceit, or social game. For how could an object be 'there' if we cannot see or hear it?

Nevertheless, there is better and worse judgement, just as there is better and worse art. What the judgement is about we are not likely to appreciate without an appropriate understanding and gaining of familiarity. A good critic does not make us reminisce, or chat about the artist's wife, or convey to us his private and idio-syncratic associations with the work. He so describes the work that we come to see what the aesthetic object is, and agree to or dissent from his judgements about it. He picks out the first and second subjects, points to modulations, draws our attention to qualities of melody and harmony. He explains the setting of a 'representational' work, for instance the religious story depicted, draws attention to movement and counter-movement, the careful distribution of figures, the effect of certain highlights, how the expression has been caught and the face modelled by the use of light and shade, and how perfect balance has been achieved without seeming to follow a rule. Yet he cannot provide us with any set of simple rules for this process of criticism, because a feature which is entirely fitting in one work would be painfully dissonant or unbalancing in another But by degrees he can lead us to a greater understanding and appreciation, and begin to develop in us some capacity for critical judgement and discrimination.

(*e*) *Ethics*. A common enough view of ethics, and one which is, perhaps, the result of a post-Victorian reaction against authority, is that it is a rather niggling set of injunctions to do with sex, charity and self-denial. But this is far from being the truth. Ethics is concerned with all human values, and with the rules, principles, standards and ideals which give them expression. In relation to action and choice, therefore, ethics must be conceded primacy over each of the forms of understanding we have so far considered. This is not to say that ethical considerations ought to bend or twist the findings of science or history, or that art should be subordinated to a political requirement that it exhibit 'social realism', but it is to say that the attribution of value to the *activity* of being a scientist, historian, artist or follower of the arts is an ethical matter.

Even aestheticism, the subordination of everything to aesthetic appraisals, is itself an ethical choice. It is to say that art ought to be regarded as the highest value in human life, and that cannot *itself* be an aesthetic judgement. The necessary primacy of the ethical in relation to action and choice shows itself more clearly, however, when values conflict, as they do when scientific research requires experiments on people, when history is rewritten to glorify a party or dictator, or when works of art lead to crime. For in such cases we are forced into greater self-consciousness about the valuations to be placed on various human activities, valuations which had, perhaps, lain concealed from ourselves until the conflict arose.

Because of this primacy, ethical evaluation is one of the areas which always offers a temptation to the authoritarian to legislate for others how they ought to live, and to visit them with punishments and inconveniences if they do not comply. But of any authority we can always ask, though it may sometimes be imprudent to do so, why we ought to do what he says we ought to do. This is to ask for reasons, for statements of what makes it right, or sensible, or wise, so to act, which raises the whole problem of the validation of ethical judgements.

Asking for reasons also implicitly asserts one's autonomy, as a person to whom good reasons have to be given in order to gain compliance. Furthermore, such reasons will be reasons for anyone, other things being equal, so that the would-be authoritarian must submit himself to the same ruling which he prescribes for others. Reason, equality and personal autonomy are therefore very intimately connected concepts. To ask for reasons is to assert one's autonomy, and to submit to reason is to place oneself equally with others under its sway. But independence of authority in no way precludes one, of course, from choosing to avail oneself of the advice, experience and judgement of others, and doubtless we are often wise to do so.

A convenient distinction within the ethical can be drawn between social morality and individual ideal (Strawson, 1966, ch. 15). By 'social morality' here is meant the system of interpersonal regulation in terms of which certain important kinds of restraint are demanded and certain actions required. So important are these, in fact, that we often embody them in laws in order to give them precision, to emphasize their importance and to provide a remedy in case of their disregard. The general concepts involved in this sphere are those of right, wrong, duty and obligation, though there are many more specific concepts which mark out what is to be approved or disapproved in some concrete connection.

The validation of the rules of social morality is ultimately in terms of such fundamental formal principles as fairness or justice, and the consideration of people's interests or good (see Peters, 1966, part 2). Conceptions of people's interests are, of course, variable. They vary with the beliefs and local circumstances of a society, and with the particular roles in which we may be acting. One has duties as a father, as a friend, as a teacher, as a citizen, as well as more general duties not attaching to any particular social role. Some of these latter may briefly be mentioned.

Two formal principles of social morality have already been mentioned, but there are many general rules safeguarding basic interests we share. Such rules concern control over various kinds of inclinations, such as aggressiveness, greed, sexuality and intolerance of differences. These prohibit killing, injury, cruelty and the subtler kinds of hurtfulness, such as rudeness, spite and causing embarrassment; they safeguard property; they constitute roles, such as those of courtship and marriage, for the expression of sexuality; they restrict intrusion upon and interference with others.

Other rules concern not so much control over inclinations as the recognition of positive obligations to others. These include obligations towards one's children, truth-telling, promise keeping, cooperation in joint enterprises and rendering assistance to others in need. Though none of these basic rules is absolute, in that one may always be overridden by another on a particular occasion, they are together basic conditions of social life. They may be largely taken for granted in a well-ordered state of affairs, though when they are absent, life, as Hobbes said, is 'solitary, poor, nasty, brutish and short'.

But basic interests do not comprise the whole of ethical life and, granted an underpinning of basic moral rules such as those just mentioned, there is room for considerable variation in individual ideals. Concepts more characteristic at this level are those of good, bad, worthwhile, desirable, satisfaction, happiness and health. Political liberty, social justice and education are key enabling conditions for appreciating the possibilities of choice at this level. We may value, above all, family life and friendship, or the pursuit of the arts, or scholarship, or the membership of some church, or social work, or being close to nature, or being in certain company, or inventing, or risk and adventure, or some combination of these and many other valued activities. Social science, literature and history reveal to us further possibilities.

Validation here involves the negative condition of compatibility with basic morality, but beyond that, coming to see for ourselves and appreciating the descriptions under which various ways of living are to be praised, admired and perhaps chosen to be followed. Such choice is not, of course, something made in five minutes, but is rather a matter of a steady growth in understanding and gaining in conviction of the rightness, for oneself at least, of some particular way of living, some fundamentally worthwhile ideal of life.

(f) *Religion.* It might be argued that religion merits a place in the curriculum on precisely the same grounds as do the forms of understanding already discussed; for religion, it might be said, is surely an important element in understanding our situation in the world. It has its interconnected concepts, such as God, grace, sin, heaven, immortal life, damnation and, more recently, 'ultimate ground of all our being'. Again, it has what look like distinctive validation procedures in religious experience, in historical revelation through Christ and the prophets, and in the 'proofs' of natural theology. Obviously justice to these claims cannot possibly be done in a page or two, but at least a gesture is possible towards some of the issues that it raises. (For some recent discussions, see Flew and MacIntyre, 1955; Mitchell, 1957; Ferre, 1962; Smart, 1964.)

Religion, of course, is not just a matter of religious doctrines. It involves moral injunctions, rituals of worship, and institutions. Thus by combining creed, code, cult and church it presents not just one possible activity among others, but a whole way of life. Nevertheless, there is good reason for taking the credal basis of doctrine as central. It has already been pointed out in an earlier section that prayer and worship presuppose belief in God, and 'belief in' presupposes 'belief that', which in turn raises questions of *truth*. Religion is about God, moreover a God who is not just the correlate of our attitudes and aspirations, but who is 'there' whether we believe Him to be so or not. Furthermore, how can the members of a church regard themselves as offering worship to the *same* object unless there is some set of intelligible and true beliefs to furnish a criterion of sameness here?

Questions of belief and truth can, of course, be evaded. One can say that here is a mystery which places God beyond our comprehension. One can welcome paradox and be undismayed by any contradictions that may be uncovered. One can follow Kierkegaard in speaking the language of 'commitment' and of 'leaps of faith'. The effect of this is to put religion beyond the reach of rational scrutiny, but by the same token no-one is given any reason to follow in making the same commitments and leaps. Moreover, there are questions to do with the relations between belief and will here which, when raised, seem to indicate that such commitments involve a loss of integrity and a lapse into what Sartre calls 'bad faith'. One cannot *make* one's beliefs about God be true simply by energetic affirmations, or by a settled will to believe.

The reason why questions of belief and truth are evaded or by-passed by some is easy to see. Grave difficulties are involved in trying to answer them. Religious experience and historical revelation already presuppose, rather than establish, belief in God. No experience could by itself establish the existence of its supposed object, and secular history establishes only that certain people said that they had certain beliefs and experiences: it cannot validate those beliefs and experiences in religious terms. Nor do the traditional proofs stand in much better case since Kant's criticisms of them and later refinements of those criticisms. The Ontological Argument falsely supposes that the existential application of a concept can be determined without going outside a system of definitions. The Cosmological Argument at most shows that a first cause is conceivable, but from then on is the same as the Ontological Argument. As for the Teleological Argument, why should it be conceded that there is *design* in the world, or just *one* designer, or that the designer is *God*?

Further difficulties are raised by God's goodness and justice. In relation to His goodness, there is the classic objection of the evil in the world that is suffered by innocent people. Either God cannot stop it, in which case He is not omnipotent; or He will not stop it, in which case He is not good. In relation to His justice there are problems to do with human freedom and responsibility which go back to Pelagius. Either I am not able to choose the good by myself, in which case how can I justly be held responsible and punished for a wrong choice; or I am able to choose, in which case my freedom limits God's omnipotence and my nature cannot be so sinful as to need God's redeeming grace.

There are other objections which, though not in logic strictly relevant to the truth or falsity of religious claims, nevertheless seriously affect our estimates of the likelihood that certain claims would, on further inquiry, turn out to be true. These 'weakeners', rather than objections, include the following: post-Freudian explanations of religious belief in terms of wishes for security; the post-Darwinian removal of religious discourse from the field of factual claims about human origins; sociological observations on the ways in which religious institutions become vested interests and are even consciously used in the ways that Plato recommended; comparative studies showing that there are many different religions, all firmly holding their contrary doctrines to be true and often having their own stock of confirming miracles, etc. These facts, as was said, are not strictly relevant to any particular truth-claim, but they are very relevant to our estimates of the individuals who make the claims.

Prior to questions of truth or falsity, however, are questions of intelligibility. What does it *mean* to say that one 'believes in God'? Images may give the appearance of meaningfulness, but once religious notions are stripped of their anthropomorphic imagery, what is left as the object of belief? Yet stripped of such imagery they must be, for God is transcendent and to worship images is idolatry. Nor are matters helped if pictures are replaced by concepts, such as love, will, power, father and creation, for such concepts get their meaning from their *human* use, and cannot literally apply to God. They can be no more than heavily qualified analogies, but the admission of this may be judged to result in what Flew has called 'death by a thousand qualifications' (1955, 97). And why should God not be tall, fat, sulky, or impatient, only in a 'different but analogous sense', of course? Again, how is God, who is eternal, perfect and therefore *lacking* in nothing, to be related to a world which is changing in time and with which God is not satisfied? As a final strain on our credulity, how are we to conceive of our survival after death? In what sense could a disembodied soul be a *person*, capable of self-reference and of individuation from other souls?

Of course, no one of these is a decisive objection. In response to any of them further distinctions of sense can be made, arguments distinguished, analogies drawn, and possibilities held to be open. Powerful sentiments incline us to go on trying to say something intelligible and to establish its truth. We may in a certain mood be struck, as was Wittgenstein, by the *amazing* fact that there is a world at all. We may feel a debt of gratitude for being alive which searches for some object to whom to express it. We may want some way of articulating our awe in the face of the world and of life, some way of focusing our highest aspirations and of reassuring ourselves in the face of our inevitable death. We may even want to be comforted to such an extent that we wilfully silence honest doubt, and make animated attacks on anyone who disturbs us in our self-deception. Our quandary, as A. C. MacIntyre suggests, would seem to be that we cannot accept Christian theology, while at the same time it provides the only vocabulary we have in terms of which to raise certain fundamental questions about human life (MacIntyre, 1967, 69).

Thus nothing is ever finally settled here. Sensitive and intelligent people can be found on both sides. And because the claims of religion can finally be neither substantiated nor dismissed, while on the other hand *if* they are true they must be of the highest importance, we cannot presume to settle the matter on behalf of others, whatever we may decide in our own case. For these reasons it was argued earlier that children in the schools should certainly learn *about* religion, for instance in literature and history lessons, and later in lessons specifically devoted to the *discussion* of religious questions, but that it would be unjustifiable to indoctrinate or deliberately attempt to initiate, as is done by many at present. No doubt this is an uneasy compromise, but it does have regard to how things are.

Understanding and choice. It was said earlier that the exercise of rational choice presupposes a well-grounded understanding of one's situation in the world, and to elucidate this further the question was raised of what was meant by a 'form of understanding', and upon what principle such forms were to be distinguished. The question now to be considered concerns the sense in which such understanding is a basic element in choice. Certainly it is not being claimed that *all* our knowledge belongs to one or other of these forms of understanding. Primitive physical abilities, such as the knowledge of how to raise one's arm, or locate one's sensations, are not included. Nor is a great deal of our perceptual and memory knowledge. We do not need a formal education to enable us to see birds and houses, to remember what we did yesterday, or to recognize at least the simpler sorts of motivation in other people.

What is claimed is that the forms of understanding above mentioned are basic ways in which human experience has, as a matter of fact, been extended and elaborated in the course of history. Such understanding is therefore presupposed by rational choice and hence is of great relevance to formal education, of which it is in special need for its transmission. It may fairly be equated, as P. H. Hirst equates it (Hirst, 1965), with 'liberal education', or the education fit for a free man.

All but the simplest kinds of human activity draw upon these forms of understanding. The liberal professions draw on them, so do the technologies, industry and commerce. A profession such as that of the teacher, for example, draws on the human sciences and therefore on mathematics, and cannot escape having ethical views as to what is worth while. It is further illuminated by being seen in its historical perspective, while the arts and natural sciences constitute important elements in what is to be taught. Even leisure activities involve these forms of understanding. Take aqualung diving, for example. Some knowledge of the relevant sciences and of mathematics is necessary if elementary safety precautions and the functioning of equipment are to be understood. Aesthetic and scientific elements, and even obvious historical ones, enter into the object of the activity and supply it with the value placed on it as part of a chosen way of life.

These forms of understanding, then, are central to human culture. They do not all enter in explicit detail into every choice that
anyone ever makes, but they are constitutive of important aspects
of one's general situation in the world, indeed in many ways can
alone disclose what 'the world' *is*. Not surprisingly, therefore, those
who would regulate the lives of others in defence of privilege and
selfish interest are always suspicious of widespread education and
seek to limit it to themselves.

This was one aspect of our own elementary school tradition. The
lower classes, Robert Lowe said, ought to be educated to discharge
the duties cast upon them. Of course, this was all represented as
fitting people, not so much for suitably menial roles and impoverished lives, as for the station to which it had pleased God to call
them. Holmes, writing in 1911, comments reassuringly on an
upper-class lady's alarm at witnessing properly educational activities in an infant school, for if this went on, she said, where were
the servants to come from? (Holmes, 1911, 228 fn.) And the activities of dictators in relation to universities are well known. Even
though education may not make the defence of selfish privilege
impossible, since one can always coerce, it does make its defence
much more difficult.

Understanding and the emotions. The fourth and last point raised
for elucidation concerned the relation of the emotions to understanding. Imagination and critical thinking are linked in obvious
ways with the development of such understanding, but the emotions might be thought not to be. There is, indeed, something of a
traditional opposition between reason and emotion (see Warnock,
1957; Peters, 1961; and Kenny, 1963, on the concept of emotion).

We are invited to think, on the one hand, of the 'rational' person,
who is cold and calculating and who has an arid and detached
intellect conceived of as some kind of instrument, while the
'emotional' person, on the other hand, is warmly responsive, immediate in his feelings, spontaneous and sincere, even if sometimes
misguided in his sincerity. It is, perhaps, worth noting that this

opposition seems to be one strain in the hostility between 'formalists', who want to 'prepare them for life', and those child-centred theorists who see salvation to lie in the spontaneity and immediacies of play. Whether either of these two has an adequate concept of emotion may be doubted.

Plainly the emotions have an inner, feeling-side to them, and one which is difficult to describe except by metaphor. To convey what we mean here we use hydraulic metaphors, such as swelling, rising and falling, metaphors of pressure, such as venting and containing, and cooking and burning metaphors, such as boiling, simmering, flaring up and dying down. But, equally plainly, the emotions are not just a matter of such feelings, otherwise they would be no different from bodily sensations such as heartburn, indigestion and vertigo. Whereas bodily sensations have bodily causes which we may or may not be able to discover and remove, the emotions are linked to objects and states of affairs which are seen in a certain evaluative light. It is this difference which holds promise for the emotions of being to some degree educable, whereas sensations are not. To illustrate: I am angry with Jones *because* I see him as thoughtlessly frustrating my purposes; I am joyful over the news *because* it is such a relief after what I had expected; I am proud of the rockery *because* its configuration successfully embodies my intended design for it.

It is not simply in terms of frowns, breathing, movements, smiles, shouts and blushes that we know what someone is feeling, but also in terms of our knowledge of the light in which he sees his situation. The link between what we feel and the evaluative light in which we see the situation is not just a contingent but a logical one. I logically could not feel certain emotions unless I saw the situation in an appropriate light. What I felt on winning ten thousand pounds could not be 'fear' unless I saw the situation as involving a threatened loss of friends, a temptation to corruption, or something similarly harmful. Again, what I feel when I look at the sky could not be 'pride' unless I see it as being my fine achievement, as I might do if I were a god. Thus the various concepts of the emotions involve a logical connection between how the situation is seen and what we may say is being felt. This is one way in which the opposition of reason to emotion can be misleading, for both perception and evaluation are a necessary part of emotion.

An interesting consequence of this logical connection is that there are many emotions which young children just could not feel, because they lack the necessary understanding to see the situation in the appropriate light. A one-year-old could, in general, have no regrets, and certainly could not feel remorse, for both regret and remorse presuppose concepts of the past and of oneself as a responsible agent identical through time. A five-year-old could, in general, have no fears or anxieties about political decisions, simply because he lacks as yet the relevant concepts of government, authority and social consequence. An eight-year-old could not, in general, share Kant's particular admiration and awe for 'the starry heavens above', because he would lack the relevant knowledge of Newtonian mechanics.

Emotional 'development' is not simply a matter of cognitive development, of course, but neither could it be just a growing inner turbulence and agitation. Emotional development is the encouragement, refinement, direction, control and sometimes suppression of feelings in the light of certain evaluations of them. Emotions can be worthy and unworthy, justified and unjustified, warranted and uncalled for, all of which shows an intimate link between emotional development and ethical understanding (see Williams, 1965).

The education of the emotions may include, according to our ethical evaluations, the encouragement and refinement of compassion, love, regret, excitement, gratitude, self-respect and pride in achievement. It may include the encouragement of a proper degree of anxiety over real dangers, such as crossing roads, leaving objects about that cause injury, and touching exposed electric wires. Certainly it will include fostering the emotions which sustain mathematical, scientific, historical and aesthetic activities, and which accompany the kinds of critical appraisal internal to these forms of understanding.

Another aspect of the education of the emotions will be the negative one of suppressing, by self-control and foresight of consequences, undesirable emotions such as hatred, malice and unwarranted anger. Alternatively, the situations that give rise to such feelings may be met by forming appropriate habits for dealing with them, though doubtless better than either would be a development of understanding which altogether dissipated such feelings, where this is desirable.

Far from there being an unavoidable opposition between reason and emotion, therefore, one can see many connections through the fact that the concepts of the emotions logically connect feelings to evaluations. To consider more particularly the basic forms of understanding that we distinguished, one can see that the ethical is central in emotional development. Yet the others enter too, partly in that the activities associated with them require and refine feeling, and partly in that they have important applications to do with truth and falsity about the object of the emotion, as in showing something really to have, or really not to have, certain important properties, or consequences for us.

Nevertheless, it must be admitted that there is some basis for the familiar opposition. The emotions are realities which may interfere with perception, memory and reasoning in many ways. They may lead us to misrepresent in order to legitimize a desire to hurt. They may impulsively prompt us into action we later regret and could have avoided had we only paused first to consider the implications. They may be appealed to and played upon by demagogues in a deliberate attempt to disrupt or break down rational processes of thought. But these are aspects of the pathology of the emotions and do not concern their education. Nor could a general justification for the disruption of reason by emotion ever be given, since such a justification would already presuppose a commitment to reason inconsistent with its depreciation.

VALUES AND THE PRIMARY SCHOOL CURRICULUM

We are now in a position to draw together the argument so far and to make a general statement of aims for primary education in terms of the curriculum to be adopted. Two brief points need to be made before actually doing this, however. First, there are no aims of *primary* education. There are only aims of education which are to be pursued in a manner appropriate to the primary *stage*. The second point is that the determination of what it is to pursue such aims 'in an appropriate manner' involves highly complex practical judgements (see Hirst, 1966, ch. 2).

Involved in the making of such judgements are the architectonic values which give direction and point to the enterprise, questions of logical priority within each form of understanding, general psychological and sociological considerations and, not least important, a multitude of factors to do with individual children, their ages, abilities and interests, and to do with administrative matters such as premises, staff abilities and experience, and material resources available. Even in moving from our arguments on values and the curriculum to a statement of intermediate aims for the primary school, we shall be making many assumptions of an empirical, though general, kind. These empirical assumptions, however, may not unreasonably be taken to be uncontroversial.

Curriculum content. From a review of the two solutions to the problem of curriculum construction mentioned on page 60, it would seem that the content or matter of the primary school's activities could conveniently be conceived of under three main headings, each of which merits some very brief discussion. To begin with, there would be the first four of the basic forms of understanding that were discussed: mathematics, the sciences, history and the arts.

Regarding the sciences, there would seem to be no justification for distinguishing, within a simple experimental, observational and mathematical approach, between the different natural and human sciences in which interesting work might be done. At some stage in the primary school, children would touch upon what *we* know to be physics, chemistry, biology, meteorology, geology, astronomy and physical geography. On the human side, they would similarly touch upon elementary anthropology, economic geography, and some aspects of the psychology and physiology of perception. They would also do some local community studies within the same observational and mathematical approach.

If by history is meant the construction or reading of historical narrative, then this would seem generally to be beyond the grasp of primary school children, but much could be done of a concrete kind to do with social, military and industrial history, sometimes with reference to the local area and its museums and relics. Again, fragmentary contributions towards the growth of historical understanding will constantly be made incidentally, as in examining an old coin that has been brought, explaining the dating system, explaining the etymology of words, reading *Robinson Crusoe* and the like.

Just as there seems little point in making divisions within the general form of science, so too with the arts there seems no justification for sharp divisions, though some will be dictated by differences in the materials used and by convenience in distributing the usually uneven talents of staff. Within the form of the aesthetic would occur poetry, creative writing, drama and 'stories', singing, instrumental music and dancing, painting and drawing, sculpting in clay and making pottery. There are two great advantages to recognizing the common aesthetic nature of these activities. First, attention is directed onto the activities themselves, so that they are not regarded just as opportunities for doing something else: poetry as a geography lesson, drawing as a chance to do some more geometry, or painting and drama as occasions for some lay psychoanalysis, for example. Secondly, in so bringing them together it is much less easy to depreciate or ignore them, as unwitting perpetuators of the elementary school tradition are apt to do, in a too exclusive pursuit of English and arithmetic, perhaps.

Of course, to show the value of mathematics, the sciences, history and the arts is not sufficient to prescribe a syllabus. Many sub-criteria would be necessary to do that, together with an acquaintance with each of the forms of understanding involved. Such sub-criteria might include: (i) logical priority, as with mathematics very noticeably; (ii) utility for some other part of the curriculum, as with the 'basic skills'; (iii) economic value, as with mathematics and science; (iv) relevance to and exemplification in our own particular form of social life, as with history and the arts; (v) the particular interests of individual children, or the special abilities and knowledge of members of staff.

The second heading under which curricular content could conveniently be conceived is that of the 'basic skills' already mentioned. These would include the 'mechanics' of reading and writing, and perhaps learning to speak a foreign language, or learning English in the case of immigrants and some English children. Included also would be certain *constantly reviewed* procedures in arithmetic which are of such utility both socially and for other parts of the curriculum that a high level of proficiency is required in them. Perhaps also map-reading ought now to be regarded as a basic skill. Under this heading too would come the gradual training in the presentation of work which is publicly legible and intelligible. There is point in J. Barzun's comment that 'the teacher may be right to begin by saying "Never mind spelling, write eagerly and quickly", but he goes on saying it so long that in the end orthography is an offence in the nostrils of the "gifted" ' (Barzun, 1959, 258).

Before leaving the 'basic skills', however, something more ought to be said on the crucially important question of reading. Reading, of course, is something more than proficiency at phonic analysis and word recognition, essential though these are, for a person has not read a book if he has done no more than recognize every word in it. One could do that going through the book backwards. By 'reading' is meant the grasping of an appropriate meaning from a text, though admittedly on the basis of continuous word-recognition, since otherwise one might simply be guessing correctly.

But what is an 'appropriate' meaning? This question cannot be answered in any definite way without further specification of the text, and here an important point emerges. The books which a child first learns to read use language and concepts with which he is already thoroughly familiar, but the books which he reads later introduce him to new words and concepts. Once he has learned to read, he can read to learn, and this learning will involve him not just in some undifferentiated 'reading for information', with its rucksack view of knowledge, but in the different forms of understanding. This is an important point if one is to be clear just what a 'reading lesson' is supposed to be at various stages (see Dearden, 1967a).

Being able to read is a crucial condition of progress in education itself. Books free the child from dependence on the patience and availability of others and enable him to go ahead on his own and when he likes, in school and out of it. Again, books and cards are an important medium of instruction, especially if teaching is to be done in groups, or individually. Furthermore, a child who cannot read is necessarily a child who cannot write, so that any kind of creative or factual writing is barred to the non-reading child. So important is reading, in fact, that one would have thought it an unquestionable *presumption* for anyone concerned about children's education at all, that children would begin learning to read at the earliest opportunity. Such a presumption might admittedly be defeated in the case of clear indications of 'unreadiness' of the non-ideological kind distinguished in the previous chapter.

The third convenient curricular heading would be physical education. This would include activities of a gymnastic kind, team games involving ball skills, co-ordination and co-operation with others, swimming, some athletics and also incidental health education, though many points to do with health could well serve as sub-criteria in the choice of topics for investigation in science. These, then, would be the three main curricular headings indicated by our discussion of values. What extra-curricular activities a school might arrange, such as chess, stamp, art and craft clubs, and competitive field games, would surely be an optional matter for the children and staff alike.

Procedural values. The fifth basic form of understanding, the ethical, would, granted certain empirical assumptions, seem best to enter into primary education through other activities of teaching and learning, rather than as a formally structured piece of learning by itself. Procedures of teaching should have respect for personal autonomy, but at the same time without depreciating other values in one-sided adulation of 'the child'. Autonomy gains in value with every increase in understanding and appreciation of the basic constitutive elements in rational choice. This poses for the individual teacher problems of judgement which are certainly insoluble in general terms. Moral education would be ingredient, therefore, in the procedures of teaching, with fairness and the consideration of individual interests as the formal moral principles validating such rules as have explicitly to be made. However, much could remain implicit as a general climate of expectation regarding acceptable standards of behaviour.

Beyond such a basic social morality, the ethical includes a multitude of more or less divergent ways of life and possible self concepts. Here, on the view for which we have argued, the teacher's task is not that of firm insistence so much as of disclosure, unaccompanied by subtle and unsubtle pressures towards compliance. This could take place through history, including the history of religion, literature, including religious literature, and the human sciences, which even reveal ways of life in contrast to anything at all found in our own society.

Two final aspects of the ethical in relation to procedures and the curriculum need to be mentioned. It may be thought valuable at the primary stage to attempt something by way of sex education. If so, it is important to be clear what one is doing. Is 'sex education' simply to be taken as a perhaps embarrassing piece of human biology, or are certain values involved in intimate personal relationships to be discussed? In short, is 'sex education' to be science, or ethics, or both? If it is to be ethics, is the line to be drawn at minimal moral observances, or are complete prescriptions to be issued as to how to conduct oneself? The difficulty with the ethical aspect is that both basic moral restraints and legitimately more divergent valuations of personal relationships are involved.

The other aspect of the ethical just mentioned and still left for consideration concerns 'mental health'. The meaning of the term is somewhat unstable, but it can be given a useful one in terms of the psychological conditions necessary for education to succeed (see Peters, 1964b, ch. 2). Such conditions would include security, confidence and trust. Some degree of psychological insight would be necessary if the teacher was to be sensitive to such needs and to be able to identify children in need of referral for more skilled treatment from the child guidance clinic, if the local authority had awoken to the need for one.

ORGANIZATION AND METHODS

Before actually making any comments on organization and methods, it might be worthwhile to indicate briefly some of the points of detail on which the curriculum design suggested above differs from the content of the traditional curriculum. Differences of principle and priorities of value have of course already been sufficiently discussed at length.

First of all, religious instruction, prayer and worship would disappear, though there would be incidental teaching *about* religion, in literature, history and social studies, for example. Secondly, 'English' would disappear as a unitary subject. Instead there would be basic language skills and the forms of aesthetic education that use language as a medium. Some traditional aspects of 'English', such as 'comprehension', would disappear altogether as exercises isolated from the comprehension of something which had a justifiable place of its own, such as history or science. Whether 'grammar' would be retained would depend on how valuable the systematic study of a language was thought to be at the later primary stage.

Thirdly, 'geography' would be explicitly recognized to be a loose federation of natural and human sciences, and investigated as such, while map-reading would be regarded as a basic skill, important both for history and geography alike. Finally, 'craft' presents certain puzzles. In part, this has in the past consisted of defunct handicrafts for boys and needlework for girls, both of which had an important place in the strictly utilitarian elementary school. But what is their place now? Granted the resources, something might be made of them as 'domestic skills': gardening, carpentry, cooking and needlework. This would be valuable on the social grounds mentioned in our first solution to the curriculum problem, and scientific and aesthetic elements could enter quite noticeably. But unless such a determined attempt were made to get something of value from 'craft', it would seem better to exclude it altogether from an already crowded curriculum, and to assimilate its frequent ancillary functions in relation to mathematics, history and the arts into those parts of the curriculum themselves.

To turn now to some few general remarks on organization and methods—remarks which do not strictly follow from the argument, but which rather express practical judgements made in the light of those arguments—the first point is that the teacher in the changing primary school is going to have to know much more, and himself be much more highly educated than his elementary school predecessor. The Plowden Report is well aware of this (para. 961). The curriculum courses in colleges of education will have to be stiffened and more in-service training and refresher courses provided.

To some extent, the polymathic demands on the primary school teacher can be met, as they often are already, by informal semi-specialization. In this way the basic class-teacher organization is retained, but the special interests, knowledge and abilities of some members of staff are made more widely available, in exchange for a similar relief in the other direction. Some of the arts and physical education have often been arranged in this way. Another recent idea very relevant to junior schools is for certain teachers to relieve the headteacher of the now impossible task of keeping abreast of everything, and of writing syllabuses for all subjects, by becoming 'consultants' to the staff as a whole on some particular branch of the curriculum. Such teachers would make it their business, and be paid to do so, to keep abreast of publications and developments in their particular field.

As regards schemes of work, if progression is to be assured and the work of separate teachers concerted, as surely should be done, then general schemes will need to be worked out, though the application of them to particular classes would need to be flexible enough to allow for variations in ability and for capitalizing on valuable new interests. Between the rigid, minute-by-minute timetable of the elementary school, and the 'free day', the solution appropriate to our own curricular design would seem to lie in the 'blocked' timetable, with large periods at the teacher's disposal within which to arrange activities under the main curricular headings as he thinks fit. To have some sort of timetable ensures a just balance of activities, prevents long-term aims from being lost sight of, and makes clear the kinds of appraisal of work that are relevant.

The development of the basic forms of understanding is a long-term process, but if an interconnection of concepts and an appreciation of validation procedures are to be gained at all, it would seem likely that this will only be done if this is a clear, intended and deliberately sought objective. It certainly will not 'just come'. Yet objection may be made to this, rather curiously, on the grounds that such distinctions are 'foreign to the child'. We have sought to show that they are not at all arbitrary, like some divisions of 'subjects', while to *expect* children to be already aware of what they have never been taught, and as a condition of teaching it, is as near to self-contradiction as makes no matter. Nor is it that rigid separations and exclusions are being suggested. One form of understanding often enters into another, but in a properly subsidiary role. In making a historical drawing, say of a galleon, aesthetic considerations are relevant, but ought to be subordinated to an appropriate degree of historical accuracy, or else history becomes a pretty little phantasy. Again, mathematics enters into most things, and there is no suggestion that it should not. Aesthetic considerations come into the basic skills, as when italic handwriting is taught, and so on. However, it may be admitted that these distinctions will be more important at the junior than at the infant stage.

How teaching should be organized and what methods used, whether class, group or individual instruction should be given, are questions which raise a host of considerations in addition to those to do with aims. Some discussion of such procedural concepts as play, experience, activity, self-expression and creativity will be offered in subsequent chapters, but the only general remark that would seem worth making at the moment is to deplore being doctrinaire. Whatever its merits, any single method of approach is likely soon to pall.

We have tried in this chapter to present and defend a general view of aims, given in terms of a curriculum and some general procedural principles, to give structure and direction to the complex enterprise of educating. In the light of the values thus set out, many needs-statements could be made. Many statements could also be made concerning children's interests, and indicating what new interests might be worth stimulating. Furthermore, content could now be given to such notions as 'all-roundness', 'whole person' and 'personal growth'. These seem to be gains which, if validly argued, show to be unjustified Plowden's pessimistic references to aims as being only 'expressions of benevolent aspiration'. But of course they are not free from generality, nor would it be desirable that they should be if they are to retain an overall, directive function.

Chapter Five

PLAY AS AN EDUCATIONAL PROCESS

HISTORICAL INTRODUCTION

Play, thought of as an educational process, has a long history in Western education. Plato saw it as the best way to begin children's education, on the grounds that any other way at that stage would involve compulsion, which was unbefitting for a free person. What advocates of play often miss when they quote Plato, however, is that he also saw in its freedom of activity the opportunity to detect the child's nature. Play gave the chance of seeing whether he was a child of gold, silver or a baser metal, and hence of seeing into which social class and role he was to be slotted and in which skills he was to be trained (*Republic*, 536e; *Laws*, 643c).

Much later, Friedrich Froebel saw educational significance in play too. His views have been historically important for the child-centred movement in English education. He was responsible for introducing such apparent paradoxes as that 'play is a serious business' and that 'play is the child's work'. Writing of childhood, he said that 'play at this time is not trivial, it is highly serious and of deep significance' (Froebel, 1826, para. 30). The 'deep significance' which made it all such a serious business is explained by his seeing play as an unfolding of the divine 'essence' of the child, whose activities were symbols to be interpreted only by those acquainted with certain mysterious 'laws of development'.

The old elementary school was quite clear about play. It had no business there. Children came to school to work, to 'get down to it and no nonsense'. At the most, some brief intermissions of 'playtime' could be allowed, as concessions to animal spirits and as a recuperation for the next bout of work. The dominant polarity, at least for the working classes who used these schools, was that of labour and amusement, and clearly schoolwork should not be amusement. Not only play but also art was highly suspect. In the nineteenth century the artist was often regarded as being 'little better than an impostor who demanded ridiculous prices for something that could hardly be called honest work' (Gombrich, 1966, 379). The 'basic skills' were the elementary school's main business.

With such a polarity operating, it was natural that those in revolt against authoritarian instruction should have looked to the other possibility, and tried to rescue play from its almost immoral status as amusement. This revolt set up a still-continuing child-centred tradition of eulogizing play and depicting the only alternative to it as a fiercely insensitive, jack-booted 'formalism'. The *locus classicus* for this kind of polarized reaction, however, surely lies much earlier in Rousseau's *Emile*, where the alternative to play is described as follows (Bk. 2):

The hour strikes, the scene is changed. All of a sudden his eye grows dim, his mirth has fled. Farewell mirth, farewell untrammelled sports in which he delighted. A stern, angry man takes him by the hand, saying gravely, 'Come with me, sir', and he is led away. As they are entering the room, I catch a glimpse of books . . . The poor child allows himself to be dragged away; he casts a sorrowful look on all about him, and departs in silence, his eyes swollen with the tears he dare not shed, and his heart bursting with the sighs he dare not utter.

The way to an education was to be the 'play way', for 'let us remember that without interest there is no learning, and since the child's interest is all in play it is necessary, whatever the matter in hand, that the method be a play-method' (Caldwell Cook, 1917, 3–4). Here, in Caldwell Cook's *The Play Way*, can be found the source of a persisting confusion of terms, for it is clear that by 'play' all he *means* is doing something with enjoyment and interest: 'for by play I mean the doing anything with one's heart in it' (op. cit., 4). But to assume that because play is enjoyable and interesting, therefore everything enjoyable and interesting is play, is to commit almost the first fallacy learned by a student of elementary logic, that of illicit conversion.

There also grew up a number of 'theories' of play, such as Karl

Groos's theory that it was a preparation for later life, and Stanley Hall's theory that it was a recapitulation of the stages in the evolution of a species. The psychoanalyst also had interpretations of play to offer. But such theories as these, as Margaret Lowenfeld said, 'cannot be taken to cover more than a certain part of the total field of children's play' (Lowenfeld, 1935, 36). Actual hard evidence on the educational value of children's play is hard to find, and not always favourable, so that it is not surprising to find in the Plowden Report's discussion of nursery schools that the weight of their recommendation rests, not on research, but on the evidence of a group identified as 'experienced educators' (Plowden Report, paras. 302–303).

In view of the paradoxes and confusions which have been introduced into the child-centred tradition of eulogizing play, there would seem to be some merit in unscrewing one's fixed attention from this tradition a little, and trying to determine some general meaning for the term as the name for some activities among others within a form of social life. This step may also have the merit of enabling a link to be made between the present discussion and the arguments which have been presented in earlier chapters of this book. The first task, then, is a conceptual one, to be followed by a discussion of the 'theories' of play and of play as a possible educational process. The muddles that have resulted from hurrying past the preliminary labour of clarification are only too evident.

THE CONCEPT OF PLAY

An immediate difficulty that presents itself in trying to pick out and demarcate the activities we call 'play' is their immense variety, even when one has set apart the multitude of idiomatic uses of the word. Children's play may comprise: (i) gross physical activities, such as running and climbing; (ii) manipulative activities with sand, water and bricks; (iii) impersonation, either by the children themselves, as in 'mothers and fathers', or by their toys; (iv) quite strictly rule-governed games, both for the table and for outside, such as Piaget's classic case of marbles and a range of increasingly elaborate games leading up to those of adults (Piaget, 1932, ch. 1); (v) verbal catches and teasings, such as the Opies described (Opie, 1959); (vi) there might finally be mentioned, though not elaborated upon, the unseemlinesses which children may get up to in their play, in order to counter any falsely sentimental idealizations of it, for this, too, is still play.

Not only are difficulties presented by the great variety of the forms of play, but there are also many borderline and transitional activities where it would be somewhat arbitrary to say whether it was or was not play. Adult games, for example, are characteristically activities which are more than play. They may be engaged in for health reasons, for business contacts (golf), for their aesthetic qualities (cricket), or for the friendships they develop, quite apart from sometimes being professionalized, and 'toying with ideas' may be a chosen way of hitting on new ones. The demarcation of which we are in search cannot, therefore, hope to be a very sharp one that would furnish a clear and unambiguous answer on the propriety of calling something play. Nevertheless, there plainly is a distinction to be made somewhere between play and non-play activities, or aspects of activities, even where children are concerned. Caldwell Cook was just wrong in thinking a child's interest to be all in play. As Lowenfeld points out, activities centred round normal physiological needs are not play, nor, one might add, are the various voluntary and not-so-voluntary involvements of children in adult activities and purposes, as in helping, going shopping and 'going out'.

Perhaps the first and most obvious thing to be said about the concept of play is that it picks out a class of activities, moreover participatory and not spectatorial activities. Play therefore presupposes an awareness of the real situation in which the activity takes place, for one cannot know what one is doing without having at least some awareness of how one stands in relation to other things. It would follow from this that babies in the first weeks of life cannot be said to play, for as yet they have no awareness of their situation. Nor can autistic children be said to play, for the same reason. Even with an ordinary child at play, his 'identification' with the role he is impersonating cannot be complete. He must retain some awareness that really he is not a father, doctor, gangster or whatever, not because it could not be otherwise, but because if it were otherwise his activity would not be play but total hallucination. It would not be a 'pretend' at all, and he would actually cut, hurt and so on. Even animals remain aware in play that they must not really bite.

Beyond this presupposition of an awareness of the real situation, the next point to be made about play is a fundamental one, and contrary to much that child-centred theorists have asserted. Play is a *non-serious* activity. Whether this assertion is more than a merely verbal contradiction of what is often said must wait to be seen until a clear sense of 'non-serious', and arguments for holding play to be non-serious, have been presented. For there may be other senses than that intended here in which play *is* serious.

Play is 'non-serious', then, in the sense that it has no ethical value. In the account of ethics given in the last chapter, two sorts of ethical value were distinguished. First, there were the basic interests with which private prudence and social morality were concerned, to do with safety, health, security and 'the ordinary business of living'. Secondly, there were what might be called the 'cultural values' involved in various individual ideals embodying our considered views as to what is a worthwhile form of life. These 'cultural values' might include friendship, religion, the pursuit of the arts, a love of nature, pitting oneself against natural hazards, scholarship, and so on. Activities instrumental to either of these sorts of ethical value, whether the moral or the cultural, would also be serious by derivation. Now play, it is suggested, is 'non-serious' *in the sense* that it has no such ethical value. What we play at is intrinsically unimportant. And this feature will be confirmed in the consequences which this statement is now shown to have.

It can now be seen that, although the impulse to play is natural, the forms which it may permissibly take are something that has to be learned as children come to understand a form of social life. Part of their coming to understand this, as has already been argued, is their coming to appreciate what is regarded as being of ethical value in that form of life, and hence their coming to appreciate the non-seriousness of play in relation to this. Corresponding to play on the one hand and to activities having ethical value on the other, there go appropriate evaluative attitudes. This shows up very clearly when these attitudes get out of step with social realities, as they may do in either of two ways.

In the first place, the non-serious attitude appropriate to play may be carried over into the ethical, in which case people are said to be 'playing' in a blaming, condemnatory sense. They are said to be 'playing around', or 'playing about', or 'just playing'. In 'playing at politics', or in indulging in spiteful, tormenting, hurting or destructive play, they are disregarding the moral seriousness of what they are doing and treating morality as unimportant. Of course, a child-centred theorist might make a definitional move here, much as Caldwell Cook did in equating 'play' with everything enjoyable and interesting. It might, therefore, be objected that *nasty* play was not 'play' at all. But this is to cut short conceptual analysis by presenting a merely stipulative definition, moreover one which is unargued and simply based on a personal preference for what 'nice' children do.

'Playing' may also be used in a depreciatory way when cultural values are treated non-seriously, though here we are beyond the interpersonal moral realm of duty and obligation. For not to take seriously the various ethical values involved in human life is to falsify one's situation. Short of self-mutilation, as by taking to drugs or alcohol, or self-alienation, as by pretending to himself that he is fully described by his occupancy of some social role, a person cannot conceal from himself that his acts have forseeable consequences, that deliberation is open to him as to which set of consequences he shall bring about, and that ultimately his projects forward into the future terminate in his death. And if he cannot conceal from himself these facts, but nevertheless does not take them seriously, does not occasionally reflect on the manner of his life or the concept that he has of his death, then notes are absent from his existence which lead one to say, depreciatively, that he is playing with his life.

This kind of playing is to be contrasted with the gradual stabilization round some set of values which is the mark of a normal, adult human being. Of course, sense can be given to the assertion that all life *is* play if we retain its contrast to the serious by translating the serious to some other, transcendent, realm, as Plato did, but the metaphysical impulse behind such a translation is beyond the scope of the present discussion. Perhaps the most fundamental issue in ethics is whether ethical values are, or intelligibly could be, grounded in some such transcendent reality, or whether we are forced to recognize that they depend on ourselves and on our partly discovered and partly created conceptions of human nature. The faith in the one can never finally allay all doubts, while the 'merely human' character of the other may seem to some to warrant despair.

But attitudes can get out of step in the other direction, too, and we may come to treat what is really ethically unimportant as if it were serious. We may come to take our play seriously. When this happens, we do not blame people so much as remind them of the realities. We reassure the frightened child who asked his father to be a lion and chase him that it was 'only play'. We remind the belligerent visiting school football team that this *is* 'only a game' And perhaps we note solemn Froebel's complete lack of any sense of humour in what he says about children at play, and wonder how he could see seriousness in *everything*, even in play.

The argument so far, then, is that play is 'non-serious', in the sense that it has no ethical value. What we play at is intrinsically unimportant. It can therefore easily be seen why people should so often have said that play is 'free', for indeed it is: it is free from the demands of the serious. We do not *neglect* our play, as we may neglect our moral obligations, or neglect to treat fundamental values with proper seriousness. Yet to say that we could not neglect our play conceals a certain value-by-contrast which play may have. We may, by saying this about play, forget Moore's 'principle of organic unities', which we do 'when it is supposed, that, if one part of a whole has no intrinsic value, the value of the whole must reside entirely in the other parts' (Moore, 1903, para. 112). Thus, although play may itself have no ethical value, a *life* which includes some play may nevertheless be enhanced in value thereby. A life of nothing but play may be unworthy of a human being, but on the other hand, 'all work and no play makes Jack a dull boy', as the popular adage has it. A philosopher, however, may perhaps be forgiven for preferring Moore's way of putting it.

Adults, then, find value-by-contrast in play. It is a relaxation, a refreshment, an enlivenment of the spirit. How can this be so? How is it possible? So far in this account of play it has been found convenient, and desirable for continuity, to approach it from directions determined by the previous chapter. But this stress on the non-seriousness of play, though correct, makes it look much too simply a negative matter. In showing how play can have value-by-contrast for adults we shall also discover what is positive in it, and that will lead on to seeing why it is the characteristic activity of childhood.

Play is *self-contained*, and this is our second main proposition about it. It is self-contained in the sense that it is set apart from the duties, deliberations and developing projects which make up the serious web of purposes of ordinary life. This seems to be what Dewey must have meant when he tried to distinguish work from play by saying that work attended more to results, had a longer time-span and was valuable for its continuity (Dewey, 1916, ch. 15). Of course, one can deliberate, concentrate, be absorbed and observe rules *within* play, and no doubt this is largely why child-centred theorists are tempted to call it serious, but the game or activity itself remains non-serious and self-contained.

This disconnection from the serious is often reflected, as Huizinga points out, in there being special places, times and objects set apart for play (Huizinga, 1944, ch. 1). Special playgrounds, recreation grounds, fields, rooms and halls are often set apart for it, if economic priorities will allow. It has its special times, or spells, with a clear start and finish set by the serious. Often it has its own special objects, its apparatus and toys, again if resources will allow. The concepts of such objects are logically connected to the concept of play, as is clearest in the case of a 'toy', for toys cannot be identified by their physical descriptions. Even a man could be a toy—to the gods. The concept of a 'toy' is that of an object having an indefinite range of possible physical descriptions but having a special play use.

To move from saying that play is non-serious to saying that it is self-contained is merely to examine the reverse side of the same coin, but it does begin to explain why we play. For the release from the serious, from duties, deliberations and the carrying forward of developing projects, is itself part of the attractiveness of play. But play also has its positive and immediate attractions, though these are often of a protean kind. We are thus led to a third proposition about play: play is immediate in its attractiveness. This, of course, is why so many speak of 'spontaneity' in connection with play, though this is not sufficient to characterize it. We may be immediately attracted by, or spontaneously interested in, all sorts of things that cannot properly be called play, such as reading a book, helping someone across the road, making some purchases, or getting on with some 'work'. But the immediately attractive features in play are non-serious ones. It may be the excitement of a chase, the struggle of non-serious contest, the exercise of wits in a game, the sensations of sliding or skating, the mounting tension of building a tower or being sought for in hiding, the pleasure of exercising some skill, or, culpably, the amusement of smashing someone's property, the cruel delight of tormenting a trapped animal, and the anticipated success in causing an accident. In the culpable cases, of course, play is culpable because really the activity is a serious matter. It is to be called play at all only because it is being *regarded* as non-serious. Immediate attractiveness, then, is the third feature of play, and no doubt it is this which leads people like Lowenfeld to say that play is 'all activities in children that are spontaneous and self-generated' (Lowenfeld, 1935, 37). But that by itself, as has been shown, is really too wide.

THEORIES OF PLAY

Without necessarily questioning the truth of the various 'theories' of play that have been put forward, we may well ask, quite generally, what job there is for a theory to do here. Plainly theories are not necessary to tell us what we *mean* by play, for if they were, then the majority of people who use the word would be uttering a senseless noise. Furthermore, it is impossible to see where the theorist would have found a class of activities to theorize about in the first place. Again, theorists do not tell us what we are aware of *doing* in playing, or what we see the point of it as being, for we already know that. If a girl playing with a doll is said to be 'learning the role of mother', or 'effecting a therapeutic release of aggression', this may be true, but it is not how she sees it. If she did see it that way, she would on that very account no longer be playing, but would be training herself for a domestic career, or doctoring herself. Finally, most theories of play do not easily fit all play, as Lowenfeld pointed out in the quotation given earlier, and also most theories of play are equally theories applicable to other activities as well.

What such 'theories' do do is to tell us, often illuminatingly, about the *functions* of some play activities. That is to say, they redescribe the activity in a sophisticated observer's way which draws our attention to what is effected, or brought about, by the play, even though the player may himself be unaware of this. For instance, children do not play just *in order to* get exercise or to strengthen their limbs, but a physiologist might justifiably point out that their play nevertheless does have this function. We might then take account of his observations in the apparatus and surroundings which we make available to children, for health and strength are good things to have. Again, a psychologist might draw our attention to the function of play in maintaining mental health, for instance in maintaining a desirable level of general vitality and in providing a medium in which to dramatize and hence assimilate unpleasant experiences, such as being in hospital. Once more, we might take account of this by seeing that children in restrictive surroundings, such as high flats, do have opportunities to play, and are not always discouraged from their fantasies, for mental health is a good thing to have as well. Some of the more elaborate descriptions of the *therapeutic* function of play may, however, strike us as being altogether too speculative, and as involving what the psychologist J. A. Hadfield calls the 'psychologist's fallacy'. This is the fallacy of forcing certain interpretations on children's behaviour in order to make it fit in with some special theory, Freudian or otherwise (see Hadfield, 1962, 12–13).

A very important possible function of play, for the educator, has not been mentioned so far. This is its possible learning function. Even quite a casual observation of children at play would seem to suggest that a great deal is unintentionally being picked up here. Physical properties are being noticed, practical skills of balance and co-ordination are being developed, social co-operation and speech of a sort are being made necessary, knacks are being imitated from others, curiosity is at work, and the child's 'life-space' is expanding. At a later stage, people may advance parallel arguments for team games in terms of the character-training which they are thought to give: courage, fairness, co-operation, loyalty, persistence and assessment of others are all required, though it cannot just be assumed that they will transfer, or even be shown in the first place, without the teacher's contrivance. Furthermore, team games readily engender divisive rivalries between the sides which may undo any good that is done.

Clearly the traditional elementary school's attitude towards play was over-simple. Not only was it too preoccupied with its utilitarian and economic priorities, but it was also involved in an error which can now be made explicit. Strictly, its logic is flawless: play is non-serious, education is serious, therefore education cannot be play, which is a fine example of a valid second-figure syllogism. But the error, we can now see, arises because what has been ignored is that play can have a serious *function*, in fact an educational function. A distinction therefore needs to be made in the first premise as follows: play, as seen by the child, is non-serious. Indeed it has to be or there would be no ground at all for calling it 'play'. But play, as seen by a psychologically sophisticated observer, may be serious, in that it can bring about many things which are both personally and educationally highly desirable, such as mental and physical health and various kinds of learning.

The elementary school ignored a whole range of 'transitional' activities, in between unsupervised play and educational activities which are both serious and regarded as such by children. But, it may be objected, was it not shown earlier that to regard serious activities *as play* was a culpable misalignment of attitudes in which one had to be reminded of the realities? Again, a distinction has to be made. The argument at that stage was concerned with play which had serious *bad* effects, whereas with educational play, the serious effects are *good*, and one will hardly wish to complain about that. Indeed one might argue, as did Caldwell Cook, that this result is a wonderful solution to the problem of motivation, for one learns, but 'the play way'. It can be seen, then, why play has been repeatedly called a 'serious business', and 'the child's work'. Such phrases do the double job of stressing the learning function of play, and getting it respectability in a world where 'honest work' is what counts with those who control the purse-strings. These phrases have also drawn attention to the continuity of development which is possible, granted certain important conditions to be mentioned later. This is the continuity of development from natural curiosity, fascination by pattern and colour, and transitory friendships, to the more deliberate, disciplined and sustained activities which constitute ordinary life.

Yet even on purely educational grounds two doubts may remain, especially where children of compulsory school age are concerned.

(The nursery school never had an elementary tradition from which to free itself.) The first doubt concerns the propriety of calling an educational activity 'play' when the teacher is actively and directly teaching as part of it. For we learn that 'if play activities are to be used for fully educational purposes the teacher must be an active participant in them when possible, acting as interpreter and instructor while the activities are in progress' (Brearley and Hitchfield, 1966, 24). In a way, this is a 'merely verbal' worry, though not entirely. It has what might be called 'public relations' implications for those who *only* know that 'play' is going on. It also helps to perpetuate a certain child-centred tradition, discussed in the chapter on growth, which sees play semi-mystically as a total unfolding 'stage', so that children *must* play at that stage, even if they are 'ready', in any non-ideological sense, for something more deliberate and structured.

The second doubt is more important. The assertion that play has an educational learning function, which justifies expensive apparatus, materials and qualified staff, must be able to meet two challenges, one empirical and one epistemological. The empirical challenge is to produce some hard evidence that play *does* do the things that it is said to do, so that we do not simply have to rely on unidentified groups of 'experienced educators', some of whom may be involved in versions of Hadfield's 'psychologist's fallacy'. The epistemological challenge is less hard-edged but still important. It is this: *could* the basic forms of understanding, which it was argued ought to be at the heart of the curriculum, be developed by an unintentional 'picking up', or even by a seemingly casual insinuation of oneself into children's spontaneous activities? Are there not *necessary* limits to the 'play way', valid though that might be for some kinds of learning and at certain early stages of learning? The empirical question is not one for a philosopher to try to answer, while to attempt to answer the epistemological one would require a scrutiny of the concept of 'experience'. To such a scrutiny we shall now turn.

Chapter Six

LEARNING AND EXPERIENCE

VERBALISM AND EXPERIENCE

One of the fundamental criticisms levelled against the elementary school by many theorists has been that what children were expected to learn there had little or no connection with their actual experience. This criticism is far from being just a psychological one. It is that too, of course, for the elementary school tended both to ignore individual differences in learning, and to disregard the qualitative differences involved in mental development, from child to adult. But from our point of view the criticism is primarily epistemological and ethical.

It is epistemological because, as has already been argued, what was gained from such a schooling was not an understanding but a collection of information and recipes gained by memorization and drill. Sometimes it would have been over-generous to speak of information, because even to acquire information requires that the words used be meaningful, which was not always the case. Learning such rigmarole as that 'nature abhors a vacuum', or that 'the terrestrial core is of an igneous nature', is not even to gain information. Nor is learning that 'area is length times breadth' acquiring more than a dubious and precarious facility in rearranging symbols. Such learning as this has aptly been dubbed 'verbalism'. As to the ethical objections to the elementary tradition, these are by now familiar. It was authoritarian in its ethos, and its curricular content was of little more than narrowly utilitarian value. What was to be believed was so just because someone said so, not because it was seen to be true or shown to be reasonable. Such an illiberal mode of instruction is a violation of autonomy in respect of understanding.

At least the programme for a major reform was presented in the second Hadow Report of 1931. A. N. Whitehead's 'inert ideas' were rightly deplored, being here defined as 'ideas which at the time when they are imparted have no bearing upon a child's natural activities of body or mind and do nothing to illuminate or guide his experience' (H.M.S.O., 1931, para. 74). Dewey would have said 'ideas with no interaction or continuity'. Contrary to the current practice, therefore, the 1931 Report recommended that 'the curriculum is to be thought of in terms of activity and experience rather than of knowledge to be acquired and facts to be stored' (para. 75). The 1959 Handbook repeated this (H.M.S.O., 1959, 7–8) while in 1967 the Plowden Report saw no reason to dissent from it, but rather spelled it out in terms of methodological innovations made since 1931.

From this stress on experience have sprung the various 'audiovisual aids' to teaching, such as broadcasts, films, visits, plentifully illustrated books and living things in the classroom. From it too have come such methodological notions as 'providing experiences', 'structured environment', 'stimulating environment', 'structural apparatus', and also major architectural changes in school building, with the outside world sometimes only too clearly visible through the large, low-level windows. School architecture reflects theories of knowledge, amongst other things. But while it is not to be doubted that there is much that is good in all of this, doubts do arise when the notion of experience is regarded as being quite unproblematic. For can experience simply be regarded as the product of coming into contact with a plentiful supply of things? 'Let the senses be the only guide to the first working of reason. No book but the world, no teaching but that of fact' (Rousseau, 1762, bk. 3). But what is fact? Which environment is 'the' environment, or the one that is to be stimulating, or structured? Can one literally *provide* experiences?

We may need actually to do some Piagetian experiments, or actually to be caught by some of the psychologist's perceptual illusions, before we are shaken out of a naïve sense of the obviousness of what we experience, and shaken into a realization of its relativity to us as experiencers. The baby reaches for the aeroplane and sees no danger in being on the edge of the bed. The man born blind but later given his sight by the surgeon's skill does not find himself in our familiar world, with everything thoroughly obvious, but finds himself making gross mistakes. As P. Winch puts it: 'The concepts we have settle for us the form of the experience we have of the world. . . . The world *is* for us what is presented through those concepts. That is not to say that our concepts may not change; but when they do, that means that our concept of the world has changed too' (Winch, 1958, 15). Knowing nothing of symphony construction, we hear only noise. Knowing nothing of glaciation, we do not see the moraine, striations or erratics. Even something as 'simple' as horizontality is apparently not to be detected by pre-school children in the surface of liquids in tilted containers. But if the scope of our experience is determined by what we have learned, by the concepts that we have acquired, then how shall a child 'experience' mathematics, science or history in his surroundings? These achievements of long inquiry do not lie wide open to view. It is rather as Oakeshott says: 'To initiate a pupil into the world of human achievement is to make available to him much that does not lie upon the surface of his present world' (Oakeshott, 1967, 161).

THE CONCEPT OF EXPERIENCE

To 'have a concept', it will suffice us to say, is to be in possession of a principle of unity according to which a number of things may all be regarded as being the same, or as being of one kind. Concepts, then, pick out features or respects which bring some unity into our experience. The ability to recognize such features or respects does not first have to be taught. Even the baby is capable of discrimination and of the recognition of 'same again', and hence is already forming primitive and subjective concepts (Bruner, 1966a, 13–15). Such an ability must also be prior to learning the names of things, for even to learn that much presupposes an ability to grasp that the teacher is doing the same thing in naming this and that, and is uttering the same sound. To have a concept, then, such as bird, bus, electrical circuit or central government, is at the very least to be able to recognize that here is the 'same again', though the principle of unity in such recognition, the features or respects of sameness, may be hard indeed to make explicit and to state.

We can 'have' concepts at very different levels of awareness, from the level of hesitant recognition when directly confronted with an object to the level of self-conscious rule-following which may follow upon acceptance of a definition. Consider the following two assertions: (i) a child able to recognize something as 'red' must already have the concept of colour; (ii) a child able intentionally to reach for a spoon must already have the concept of space. Does this, then, show that some of our most highly general concepts are actually the first to be learned, and perhaps innate? Certainly what the child is aware of is coloured and spatial, but that does not mean that he is aware of it *as* an instance of the self-consciously applied concepts 'colour' and 'space'.

To be explicitly aware, not just of a spatial object, but of it *as* spatial, and hence as the same in this respect as other visual objects, but different from sensations, thoughts and emotions, is a sophistication to which he will not attain for many years, if at all. He 'has' a concept of colour and of space only in the sense that such are implicit in his awareness. Making them explicit, and so becoming conscious of such puzzles as are posed by the idea of a limit to this 'space', or by the idea that 'colour' may be contributed by ourselves and not be 'in things' at all, are tasks beyond the scope of infancy. We might say, then, that the child 'has' primitive concepts of colour and of space, but that he cannot yet realize that he has (see Barrett, 1962).

Explicit realization and examination of the nature of some of our more problematic concepts is, however, very much the interest of philosophers. In connection with the present problem, namely that of 'experience', it is now proposed to try to get a better hold on this concept by distinguishing between three important *kinds* of concept: important, that is, in relation to the basic forms of understanding previously discussed, and to how they are to be developed in children. The three kinds of concepts will be called, somewhat but not entirely arbitrarily, perceptual, practical and theoretical. As was just intimated, these labels have been chosen for a special job, and must be taken to mean no more than they will be allowed to mean. It is not so much an accurate analysis of their ordinary meaning that is to be offered, as a stipulation for a special purpose. Furthermore, it is certainly not being suggested that *every* concept must be of one or other of these three kinds.

Perceptual concepts. By 'perceptual' concepts are intended here such concepts of physical objects and properties as those of tree, flower, dog, bird and stone, red, square, loud, hot, sticky and heavy. The class may be defined sufficiently precisely for our purpose as that of concepts the principle of unity of which is a set of manifest properties or relations. Of course, there will always be a reason why *these* particular perceptual concepts have been acquired, and perhaps marked by language, since concepts reflect interests. They do not reflect classifications somehow unavoidably forced on us by the way that the world is. Such an appearance of unavoidability may be encouraged by reflection on the fact that certain words for perceptual concepts do seem to feature in most languages. But, equally, there are certain *interests* shared by all people, for instance interests in getting food and avoiding danger.

Perceptual concepts, though hardly the publicly shared ones marked by language, must evidently be among or involved in the very first concepts in terms of which a child brings order into his experience. Babies do not passively wait until they are guided by speakers before introducing some order into their experience. As Plowden remarks, 'the child appears to have a strong drive, which shows itself at a very early age, towards activity and the exploration of the environment. He also displays curiosity, especially about novel and unexpected features of his experience. As far as can be judged, this behaviour is autonomous since it occurs when there is no obvious external motivation such as hunger' (para. 45). Put more concretely, no-one teaches him, even by example, to try soil for taste, to observe the prowling cat that has just arrived, or to explore down the teapot spout with his probing finger.

The first learning of language, with its naming of such objects as pussy, flower, bird and so on, is somewhat dubiously to be called 'ostensive definition' (Russell, 1948, part 2, ch. 2). It is far from clear that giving the conventional word-label for an already acquired concept is what is happening. Perhaps sometimes it is this, but at other times the word-labelling will also effect a modification of existing concepts, or very much more likely, it will actually be to teach a new concept. Certainly Wittgenstein has made some telling criticisms of ostensive definition as Russell conceived it (Wittgenstein, 1953, paras. 26–37).

It is all too easily assumed that a child already has the concepts marked by language, and only needs to be told the corresponding conventions of speech. But there are insoluble difficulties in understanding such an assumption. First, pointing is itself ambiguous in its intention. How is pointing at the *colour* of the ball different from pointing at its shape, size, texture or position? How, indeed, is the act of pointing itself different from just raising the arm or twitching? The difficulty is that for a full-blown understanding of the fact that I am pointing to the colour of the ball, you must *already* understand the social conventions which constitute a certain range of movements 'acts of pointing' (handlings, stretching of the index finger, nods, etc.). And you must *already* understand what a ball is and the language-game of giving the colour of a thing.

Your understanding of what I am saying is therefore inseparably enmeshed in a mass of circumstance which is only just beginning to come into view, and 'ostensive definition' must correspondingly disappear from view as a possible account of the very first beginnings of language. Nor will an account of language learning in terms of conditioning do, such as that of the psychologist O. H. Mowrer. Understanding what is said is not a *causal* matter of responsive 'behaviours' triggered off by some stimulus. It necessarily involves your grasping my intention and being right about it, and that cannot just be a matter of behavioural responses.

Perhaps the problem can be simplified a little, however, by noticing that the first learning of words, and correlative forming of concepts, is not so much *using* language as what Wittgenstein called 'preparation' for language. We gradually teach the child to recognize balls, bottles and biscuits by saying these words as we do things with these objects, and his coming to understand us is, all at the same time, coming to understand certain names, certain conventions of pointing and certain intentions in others. And even this complex piece of learning is no more than a preparation for a later participation in the use of language, as in making requests, giving instructions, asking questions, expressing attitudes and supplying information. Far from being a process of conditioning, learning a language is indeed coming to understand 'a form of life'. It may be noted, however, that this does seem to confirm our suggestion that perceptual concepts must be among or involved in the very first that a child learns. This is a point to which we shall return.

Practical concepts. By 'practical' concepts are intended concepts of what Heidegger calls 'the equipment', namely concepts of objects which physically exist but which cannot be understood apart from seeing how they function in a form of social life (see Heidegger, 1927, Div. 1, chs. 2 and 3). Examples of practical concepts would be clock, telephone, chair, money, street, handle, shop, church, table, library, clothing and window. Practical concepts with a less determinate range of physical properties would be obstacle, food, tool, and of course toy, which we mentioned in the last chapter. The essential distinguishing feature of practical concepts, however, is that to understand them one must grasp what people *do* with an object, what they *use* it for. With perceptual concepts this is not necessary.

The application of a practical concept presupposes the application of perceptual concepts. A weed cannot be identified without seeing plants, nor can a handle be identified without seeing a protruding knob. In this sense then, perceptual concepts are epistemologically more fundamental, though it does not automatically follow, and probably is not true, that perceptual concepts are formed first in time, or are fully explicit in our earliest practical activities. The two sorts of concept are almost certainly in mutual involvement in the temporal order of experience and are clearly distinguishable only later. It will be important for the purposes of our analysis, however, to keep them clearly distinguished. One immediate advantage of maintaining the distinction is that it gives us a slightly different angle from which to approach language learning.

Consider a baby's 'seeing a table', which involves a practical concept. What does he see? At first, perhaps he has only a perceptual concept of an object with a certain shape and height, if indeed he perceives a unitary object at all. More likely, perhaps, he sees this object, but *as an obstacle* in his crawling, or *as an aid* in trying to stand up and walk. But he will not see it *as a table* until he grasps its function in domestic life, as something on which to work and to have meals. Similar advances have to be made with such objects as telephones, books, gloves, and so on, as he enters further into an understanding of social life: of people and their purposes.

Thus the world in which he finds himself and in which he moves about is also a world of social meanings. Learning the public language is not just learning the names of objects picked out solely in terms of physical properties, but also involves being told, or being shown, 'what we do'. The sense of all this is, perhaps, regained by us to some extent when we travel abroad, translate from a 'difficult' language, or still more when we ask of the things dug up at an archaeological site what these things are. For to answer that question we must not just look at them, but try imaginatively to reconstruct a way of life which men once had and the practical concepts which they had of their things. Again, not being too fixed in one's habits of practical conceptualization is one condition of practical ingenuity and inventiveness, and a number of psychological experiments, such as those of N. R. F. Maier, have investigated the varying readiness of different individuals to restructure in order to solve some practical problem.

Even though a baby may form certain unstable perceptual and practical concepts unguided by language, and even though we are always capable of a wealth of discriminations going far beyond the resources of our ordinary vocabulary to describe, still it must be conceded that language is of the very greatest importance in conceptual development. The use of words is something that is governed by public rules in terms of which we are taught what it is correct and incorrect to say. Of course, we do not normally teach the rules explicitly, as something self-consciously to be followed, but they are implicit in our constant correction of children as they learn language. Without these rules, there would be no 'correct' and 'incorrect', therefore no publicity, and therefore again no language.

Even the notion of a 'private' language, such as might be used for the writing of secrets in a diary, gets its sense from our understanding of ordinary public language, and must itself be public *in principle*. But in learning the public rules constitutive of the language used in a form of social life, we do not just gain an ability to speak correctly: we become able to *share experience*, and to participate in a common life, for the rules of language provide a criterion for the notion of 'same meaning' to be given application. When we speak, we 'mean the same thing', more or less, so that it is not surprising that 'communicate' and 'community' should etymologically both originate in the idea of the 'common' or shared.

Not only does language help to shape experience, but it also enables us to check our experience against that of others, and thus to have a criterion of 'real' and 'not real' going beyond our private imaginings. We can inquire if others find the same, though correspondingly now we can also mistakenly yield in our judgement to the pressure of the contrary opinion of others. Even with mastery of the public language, however, aspects of our experience may remain recalcitrant to our efforts to talk about them. How shall I describe my sensations, for example, or the feeling side of my emotions, or the precise way in which it hurts? Here the difficulty is to find a public criterion of 'same meaning'.

It has already been mentioned that language shapes as well as enables us to share experience. Our attention is moulded and directed by the forms of thought which have evolved with the language itself. But in being taught a language, we are indeed being taught, and not just having oral behaviour trained or conditioned in us by one who regards us as an organism or a thing. We are having things pointed out to us, being shown things and having them explained, and hence are being to that degree treated as persons, participant in a common social life. Moreover, those who teach us language, and thereby draw us into the common social life, themselves draw upon an elaborate heritage, and even upon a written history. For language overcomes the limitations of genetic transmission and makes possible an accumulation and recording of past experience. We do not just become one of the family: we inherit a culture. And this, too, like the possibility of checking our experience against that of others, may not all be good. For the particular culture we inherit, the traditions which we now take up, can set limits to our experience which are not human limits, but those of time, and of place, and of the actions of people who choose or do not choose to educate us. In a very important sense, therefore, the limits of my language, as Wittgenstein said, mean the limits of my world (Wittgenstein, 1921, section 5, 62).

Theoretical concepts. By 'theoretical' concepts are meant here concepts such as those which occur in the three intellectual forms of understanding that we have already considered, namely mathematics, science and history. Aesthetic and moral concepts cannot without strain be regarded as theoretical, though one can of course theorize *about* art and morals. But further discussion of these two latter forms of understanding will be reserved for later chapters. Theoretical concepts then, in the sense that we have roughly indicated, organize in highly systematic ways our ordinary, 'commonsense' experience, and in so doing greatly increase our intellectual understanding of it.

This 'commonsense' experience already has a structure, of course, but of another sort. It is structured in terms of a local spatio-temporal framework of physical objects, and a practical framework of social meanings. This practical structure may be public or private. It may be private in that each of us has his own set of purposes, and hence brings the world into a practical unity in relation to them. But it may also be public in that many things are arranged, not just with a view to our private purposes alone, but with a view to anyone's purpose. I arrange my private surroundings to suit myself, as do you with yours, but we also share a public world of streets, buses, shops, newspapers, ready-made clothes and railways which are not orientated towards the purposes of anyone in particular. This is Heidegger's world of '*das Man*': of what 'one does', or 'they do'.

But theoretical concepts restructure 'commonsense' experience in accordance with a particular theoretical interest, namely that of a particular community of inquirers. They are used in making statements which are validated by special procedures which are elaborated within each particular tradition of inquiry. Yet although theoretical concepts originate in such communities, that is not to say that they have no impact outside them. Indeed, they transform ordinary life through the new forms of control which they make possible, as is most obviously the case with the technologies and the professions, such as teaching, medicine, agriculture and engineering. It ceases to be possible to grasp what one sees and what is happening without an appropriate degree of relevant theoretical understanding. Where ordinary perceptual and practical concepts share the same word-label as concepts of theory, the theoretical may usurp the ordinary as being the 'correct' meaning of the word, especially when education is extended to all, so that all gain at least some theoretical understanding. And all of this has the closest of possible connections with what was said in previous chapters about the narrowness of the elementary school's curriculum and the general conditions of rational choice in our situation now.

Theoretical concepts are not necessarily as highly general or abstract as are 'binomial theorem', 'natural selection' and 'fall of the Western Roman Empire', which would all be far beyond the scope of normal primary schoolchildren to grasp. They may be so concrete as to seem to be merely our ordinary perceptual or practical concepts. Such concrete theoretical concepts would be: circle, graph, migration, lunar eclipse, fossil, ox-bow lake, manor house and Norman porch. But concrete as they may be, these concepts are only apparently our ordinary ones. To understand fully any one of them involves also understanding some theory, just as understanding a practical concept involves also understanding something of people and their purposes. You cannot 'just see' an eclipse, or a fossil, or a manor house, but only a diminished disc, a shell protruding from the chalk, or a building. But much more is being said than that when eclipses, fossils and manor houses are identified: elaborate conceptual networks of theory are being presupposed relating to the solar system, biological evolution and Medieval life. Even the apparently simple case of a circle involves reference to an elaborate system of definitions.

Even when a theoretical concept is labelled by the same *word* its elucidation is given only by the theory, as in such cases as fish, metal, rock, star and tide. In science, whales, porpoises and dolphins are not fish, because the concept 'fish' is defined in terms of criterial attributes found useful in an evolutionary classification of species. Again, in chemistry, 'metals' may be liquid, as is the case with mercury. To the geologist, 'mud' is a rock, because his classification reflects his theoretical interest in sedimentary deposition, and mud is a sediment. The astronomer counts the sun as a 'star', because it is chemical composition which furnishes his criterion of sameness. For a geophysicist, the concept of 'tide' is part of a theory which links sun, moon and earth together in a system of causation which leads him to speak even of land as having a tide. Thus even the most concrete observations and common-sounding labels are not merely matters of applying ordinary concepts, but essentially involve complex theoretical structures. These structures may even invite rebellion against our naïve domination by perception and insist on a 'rape of the senses', as with the scientific truth about the rainbow's end, and as with the belief that the stars are all equidistant from us, embedded in a dome.

Yet enthusiastic child-centred theorists assert that 'mathematics and science are all around us'. You have only to open your eyes and there they are. Such a belief exemplifies what Sir Karl Popper has called 'the bucket theory of mind': you have only to open your eyes and the truth will come slopping in, as it were. We might also say that such a belief exemplifies 'the fallacy of perfect obvious-ness', by supposing that what unavoidably presents itself to a theoretically sophisticated observer is there for all to see. 'Having mastered the distinction between odd and even numbers, it is a feat to remember what it was like in a mental world where there was no such distinction . . . It is as if the mastery of a conceptual distinction masked the preconceptual memory of the things now distinguished' (Bruner, 1966a, 64).

A final point worth noticing about theoretical inquiry is that it is not controlled by our ordinary preferences and aversions, but is the product of a passion to understand and to discover the truth. The zoologist is fascinated by snakes, while the biochemist may study bodily waste. On the other hand, the native who catches a coelocanth can see in this shattering find only food, more or less tasty or saleable. And most of us, who, as Heidegger points out (op. cit., ch. 3), experience the sun as an indicator of the time of day, as a source of comforting warmth and as a principal factor in the orientation of our buildings, can never quite concede that it is just another star, or that it is we who go round it. Nor, for ordinary purposes, need we concede it.

EXPERIENCE AND TEACHING

Concrete, abstract and logical priority. To have a concept, it was suggested, is to be in possession of a principle of unity according to which a number of things may be regarded as the same, or as being of one kind. In order to get a better grasp of the notion of experience in education, a classification of concepts was proposed in which perceptual, practical and theoretical concepts were distinguished and stipulatively defined. The two aspects involved in such concepts, namely their concrete exemplification on the one hand and their principle of unity on the other, must now be considered quite generally. For 'we have the concept in question only when we are both able to see a range of things as falling under the concept and also in the position to know what it is for them so to fall, what it is that makes them instances' (Hamlyn, 1967, 37–8). Or, as Kant earlier put it, concepts without 'intuitions' are empty, while 'intuitions' without concepts are blind.

The balance between instance and principle in learning is not, however, at every stage the same, and our threefold classification of concepts is able to bring this out. With perceptual concepts, so great and rich is the variety of discriminable features presented by the world that a large number of instances may be required before we can have any adequate grasp of the principle of unity involved here, and then in all probability we shall be unable to state it. Naming things for a young child often involves considerable exemplification before we are confident that an adequate concept has been attained. Not all trees are like the ones in our garden, in height, shape, or foliage, nor do all birds fly. With practical concepts the balance changes, because now we can economize by explaining the function for which the thing is to be used. And because it is in function that the principle of unity lies, a certain indefiniteness in the range of concrete exemplifications is even desirable. It leaves room for changes in fashion, for minor improvements and for radically new invention. Thus the physical appearance of cars, coats, bicycles and shops constantly changes, though these changes do not have to be anticipated in teaching the concept.

But with theoretical concepts, exemplification may be confined to a single observational test, for the weight now lies with the theoretical structure which specifies the instance. A theoretical physicist may never even enter the laboratory, but leave the grosser side of his speculations to others. The mathematician, once he has attained an insight into the logical structure of his systems, may kick away the ladder of sense-experience by which he first climbed to the beginnings of an understanding, and depart the world altogether for purer realms. If learning from experience is to be pressed upon us as an educational panacea, we ought therefore always to ask: (i) what kind of concept is involved? (ii) at what stage in the growth of understanding is the learner? For the stress that we may agree should be placed on experience will vary considerably according to how these two questions are answered.

For human beings to learn, as D. W. Hamlyn points out, is for them to acquire knowledge through experience, and if through experience, then it must be the case that in normal mental development the transition is from the more concrete to the more abstract, and could not conceivably be otherwise. Yet Piaget, in his various writings, seems to be presenting this as empirical discovery, and therefore as something which might very well have been otherwise. But as Hamlyn says concerning this 'discovery': 'One thing that he may be said to have discovered is that the subjects who at one stage employ concrete operations and only later abstract operations are indeed normal human children' (Hamlyn, 1967, 41).

To say this, however, is not to deny that actually doing some of Piaget's experiments with children may in fact be the best way of shaking oneself out of 'the fallacy of perfect obviousness'. Nor is it to deny that the actual ages at which various levels of understanding are normally reached must be determined empirically, and not by reflection alone. But these ages will be relative to a particular set of children. They will also be relative to a particular set of social and educational circumstances which may not be the same everywhere, and may not be unalterable anywhere.

Just as the concrete has an epistemological priority in the growth of understanding, so does it have a noteworthy priority of another sort. As P. F. Strawson points out, it is *ultimately* only by reference to material objects that things of other sorts, such as economic inflation or national prestige, can be identifyingly referred to. Furthermore, it is only by reference to this spatio-temporal framework of material things that we can all be said to live in a single, common world at all, and not in separate dream worlds. As Strawson puts it: 'We can make it clear to each other what or which particular things our discourse is about because we can fit together each other's reports and stories into a single picture of the world' (Strawson, 1959, 38).

One final general question concerning concepts: does the logical structure of the understanding to be cultivated determine the order in time in which things are to be learned? Are there any necessary temporal priorities here? (See Hirst, 1967, ch. 3.) That there are some such very general priorities has already been indicated in discussing concrete and abstract, but what of more particular cases? Let us say that concept X is logically prior to concept Y if we cannot understand concept Y without understanding concept X. In other words, a necessary condition of understanding Y is that one also understand X. In this way, we can say that the concept of an integer is prior to that of a fraction, distance to that of speed, current to that of resistance, human burial to that of Roman tumulus, and *some* practical concepts to *any* historical narrative. But must what is logically prior be learned first in time, say five days, ten weeks, or six and a half years earlier?

To suppose that logic alone can show that it must be so, even though psychologically it often may be so, would be to commit what may be called 'the fallacy of perfected steps'. This is to suppose that one thing must be perfectly, and not just partially, understood before one can move on to the logically next thing. In fact, of course, it might sometimes be possible to learn both together, both human burial and Roman tumulus, for example. Again, counting presupposes number concepts and measuring presupposes such concepts as 'a length', 'an area' or 'an angle', but it does not logically follow that counting and measuring must be deferred until what they presuppose is perfectly understood. In fact, to take the first case, counting may be a very good way of attaining number concepts, since the repetition of the same words may be precisely what draws attention to the numerical identities involved.

Logic alone leaves open the choice of sequential or synchronous learning, though experience may dictate the former often to be wiser, children having the limited capabilities for learning that they do have. In general, growth in understanding may more accurately be pictured, as Wittgenstein suggested, as being like learning to find one's way about a town, or perhaps as Plato suggested, like an ascent from a cave of confusing shadows into the clear sunlight. What in general it is not like is a series of perfectly clear and distinct sequential steps, which was Descartes' model.

Learning and theoretical concepts. How do things stand now with such notions as that play could have an educational 'picking up' function, or that we should 'provide experiences', or arrange 'stimulating environments'? What can now be made of 'learning from experience', or 'learning by discovery', and what about 'structured apparatus'? The distinction drawn between perceptual, practical and theoretical concepts, the elucidation of these concepts, and the following discussion of concrete, abstract and logical priority should now have put us in a position to see more clearly how these questions may be answered.

First of all, where the learning of perceptual and practical concepts is concerned, there would seem to be much to be said for 'learning by discovery', 'providing experiences' and the rest. Children can and do pick up a very great deal in this informal way: in play, by watching others, by seeing how things are used, by finding new and private uses for things. Gesell comments on the baby at eighteen months that he 'increases his knowledge by doing a great deal of watching of the social scene. Time after time during the day he interrupts his activity for absorbed inspection of the activities of others' (Gesell, 1943, 35). At this level of promiscuous learning, guided only by personal interests, 'subjects' would indeed be arbitrary. Mental 'development' at this stage is gaining an extended awareness of what is to be sensibly discriminated in the world, and gaining some understanding of one's form of social life. Much learning of this kind has no need of formal educational provision at all, but is going on all the time wherever children are awake and attentive. Where some educational guidance is provided, no doubt the best way is through a 'structured environment', as in the nursery school, or through 'investigation tables' and the like.

Stones, shells, feathers and wood are examined; what it is for things to dissolve, float, give out sounds and grow are noted; artefacts such as mirrors, springs, clocks, magnifying glasses and magnets have their physical properties explored and tested. These are riches, and whether the motivation for all this is an eager natural curiosity, or the seething of a cauldron of weird and sexual phantasies, much is learned, autonomy is respected, and 'growth' of a sort may be 'observed'. But the theoretical concepts of mathematics, science and history will not be learned in this way; nor is it more than a play with words to call such investigations 'scientific'. Books, television, interested parents and, above all, teachers who themselves possess to some degree these basic forms of understanding, will be necessary for the learning of theoretical concepts. There are perhaps three main epistemological arguments for asserting such a necessity for a teacher of some kind.

The first ground for the assertion is the degree of discontinuity between theoretical and 'commonsense' perceptual or practical concepts. Theoretical concepts are interconnected in elaborate and carefully constructed systems, and even where the same labels are used there is a shift in concept from the commonsensical to the theoretical. There is, of course, a connection in *application*, and this, it will be argued, provides the key to developing theoretical understanding while also starting from children's actual experience, as one must if verbalism is to be avoided. But in terms of *meaning* there is discontinuity. Theoretical concepts are connected in systems that have been elaborated and modified by a long tradition of inquirers, and historically they simply do not occur prior to the start of such communities, or even after such a start in societies or social classes uninstructed in the ideas so developed. They originate in and percolate out from such traditions of inquiry; they do not originate afresh and spontaneously in the individual minds of each generation of eager and curious children, granted only a suitable material environment.

Even the 'problems' in such traditions of inquiry reveal themselves only to insiders, since they grow out of the work that has previously been done. Dewey alone among the child-centred theorists seems to have seen this. 'There is no one,' he wrote, 'of whom independent inquiry, reflection, and insight are more characteristic than the genuine scientific and philosophic thinker. But his independence is a futile eccentricity unless he thinks upon problems which have originated in a long tradition, and unless he intends to share his conclusions with others, so as to win their assent and elicit their corrections' (Dewey, 1960, 80). It does not just occur to us to ask why mud is plastic, why light passes through solid glass, what the nature of combustion is, what the general conditions of flotation are, how solid things retain their shape or why three-four-five triangles have a square corner. We just accept such things, unless we have been introduced to appropriate traditions of speculative inquiry and questioning.

Dewey's practical solution to the consequent teaching problem is unacceptable. Partly this is because his pragmatism led him to see the value of understanding to lie solely in social power and control over things, so that ideas were to be regarded just as instruments. Partly it is because he was overimpressed by the origin of traditions of inquiry in practical social problems, such as war, farming, trade and industry, so that he overlooked the discontinuities to which attention has been drawn, and the interconnection of theoretical concepts in autonomous forms of under-standing. He therefore thought that you could start with ordinary practical situations, such as kitchens, gardens, building sites and tailoring, and grow outwards by unbroken continuities to the more structured experience we have called theoretical understanding. But theoretical studies kick away the ladder by which they climbed, and even turn round to 'rape the senses'. We saw this even with notions like fish, mud, star and metal. The concept of light would be another good example, where there is a shift away from the ordinary concept to that of something which is *invisible* and which travels. But in any case there would seem to be no good reason to accept the assertion that because such-and-such was the historical order of discovery, it should therefore be the order in the learning of individuals now.

But now might not this historically developed discontinuity be overcome by starting from children's questions, of which they are reputed to be always full to brimming? D. J. O'Connor gives us the answer to this : 'for a question to be a genuine one and capable of being answered, the questioner must have some idea of the terms in which the answer will be given' (O'Connor, 1957, 31–2). Of course, a question may simply express an unformulated dis-satisfaction, or only have the grammatical form of a question while really being something else, as O'Connor again points out, but a sensible questioner must *already know* what general sort of thing will count as an answer. He must already know what would be relevant and what an absurdity or evasion. A question well put, it is often rightly said, is already half answered. We might also add here that children's questions can often seem more profound than they really are, since their use of the same words invites the attribu-tion to them of the same understanding as we have ourselves.

Thus there are limits set to the questions I can ask by the know-ledge I already possess. The difficulty with developing a theoretical understanding in children is to get them to see that there are *new sorts of questions to ask*. This, again, Dewey failed to take account of in his view that problems would 'arise' in practical situations.

Thus depending on children's questions, and letting them find out the answers by discovery, are not just slow methods, but are likely also to be fatuous ones where theoretical concepts are concerned. Letting children make up their own questions in a mathematics lesson may be a good way of testing understanding of something already taught, but could hardly be a way of developing new and so far unheard of concepts. Thus the discontinuity remains, now in the guise of having to bring children to ask new and qualitatively different sorts of questions.

A third, and here final, attempt to overcome this discontinuity might be made by extending the notion of 'structured environment' and 'structural apparatus' so as to include instances of theoretical concepts, whether as wooden Cuisenaire rods for number concepts, trays of appropriate material for the concepts of current electricity, or pictures for such historical concepts as Roman tumulus, manor house, Norman keep, and Crusader. Children would then be able, it might be said, to view or handle these objects and hence *abstract* the appropriate concept. Indeed this word 'abstract' abounds in recent literature.

There are perhaps two objections to this, however. First, it is logically impossible to see something *as* an instance, example or model *of* something, unless you already know what the 'something' is. Recall the baby and 'seeing the table'. He could not see it *as* a table, but only as a bulky shape, until he came to appreciate its function in connection with work and meals in domestic life. But whereas a normal baby almost inevitably acquires the practical concept of 'table' in gradually coming to realize what is going on around him, there is no inevitable gaining of theoretical concepts. These originate in historically late and geographically still very restricted traditions of inquiry.

Secondly, abstractionism ignores the *activity* of the mind in forming concepts and in applying them to instances (see Geach, 1957, sections 4–11). It presents concept-formation, not as something that goes on in purposeful and interested agents, but as a passive, almost causal, registration on a *tabula rasa*. This was, of course, John Locke's view of the matter. But this will not do, for several reasons. Conceptualizing is not a passive registration but an activity in which something is 'seen as'. Thus the fruit in front of us may be seen as yellow, as lemon-coloured, as a pastel shade, or just as coloured, without *its* having to undergo any changes. Again, the conjunction of concepts in discourse and their application to instances both permit of appraisal as correct or mistaken, which could only be the case if these were things done. Passive registration is not correct or mistaken, but just a happening. Furthermore, where are the concrete instances to do the causing in Geach's case of formal logical concepts, such as 'and', 'if . . . then', 'or', and 'not'? Must we be confronted with instances of 'nottishness', or of 'alternativeness', in order for some abstraction to go on? If so, it would be impossible that we should ever acquire such concepts. Finally, if instances did cause concepts, it would be a matter for some empirical research to find out just what had been caused by what. It would make sense to wonder whether one's concept of 'red' might not have been caused by those patches of yellow one saw the other day. But plainly this is absurd. Instances are logically, not causally, related to the concepts which they instantiate.

Thus although we may have abstract ideas, we do not abstract them. Moreover, to suppose that we did would leave it a matter of the sheerest coincidence that people who speak the same language and share the same form of social life should also have the very same concepts. However, to link the formation of such concepts with formal and informal *teaching* within a form of social life would make the connection seem entirely unremarkable, as indeed it should be.

The liberalization of teaching. The solution to the problem of overcoming the discontinuity that we have been discussing is therefore still to be found. The suggestion of starting from children's questions, or of providing 'structured apparatus' and the like from which to 'abstract', do not overcome the difficulty. And there are, it would seem, three important reasons why we are led into this impasse. First, there is the ideological domination of the doctrine of uninstructed and natural growth, which is harmless and even apt enough where perceptual and practical concepts are concerned, but which quite ignores the different nature of theoretical concepts.

The second reason for the impasse lies in the fallacy of perfect obviousness, which results in notions such as 'abstracting concepts' and 'structured environment' being extended, quite without any sense of strain, to the theoretical studies of mathematics, science and history. Partly, no doubt, the doctrine is encouraged here by failing to check how much apparently spontaneous generation of such concepts results from out-of-school influences, such as television or interested and educated parents, and partly it is encouraged by failing to check assiduously that the supposed learning really is going on, and is not just being read into children's activities in the fervour of doctrinal enthusiasms. Of course, the theory says that detailed records should be kept. In practice one finds that to do this with forty self-directed, freely choosing children is quite impossible.

The third reason for the impasse is a reaction against the elementary school tradition which is altogether too undiscriminating. It sees everything connected with that tradition as tainted beyond redemption, no matter how liberally it may now be conceived. Yet it should not be thought that such a reaction has the wholehearted support even of psychology. To quote from a leading contemporary educational psychologist: 'mental growth is in very considerable measure dependent on growth from the outside in . . . a theory of development must be linked both to a theory of knowledge and to a theory of instruction, or be doomed to triviality' (Bruner, 1966b, 21).

Our own suggestion as to how theoretical subjects should be introduced, and at least a start be made in developing the appropriate forms of understanding, is that a liberalized conception of teaching is needed. But to begin with, let it be clear that nothing like the elementary tradition's narrow curriculum is intended here.

A view as to what the curriculum of the modern primary school should be has already been presented in chapter four. Furthermore, there is no necessary implication here of *class* or *formal* teaching, though there is surely some place for both of these. Instruction can be given to groups or individuals, and it can also be given informally through giving out cards or by referring to books (see Dearden, 1967b, ch. 9).

Teaching the basic forms of understanding cannot, consistently with the kind of achievement being aimed at, be authoritarian, though it could be a little too forceful and obtrusive for some tastes in these matters. For the kind of teaching which is appropriate to such an aim 'may be characterized as an activity aimed at the achievement of learning, and practised in such a manner as to respect the student's intellectual integrity and capacity for independent judgement' (Scheffler, 1967, 120). On this side of the Atlantic we do not normally refer to children as 'students', of course, and Scheffler is concerned with the ultimate aim, not the very beginning, but his statement makes the point well.

Coming to understand for oneself is coming to grasp impersonal validation procedures and to share public concepts, and hence is at once a gain in independence of others and an entering into community with them. Reason, equality and dignity are, we earlier followed Kant in arguing, very intimately connected concepts. Teaching of the kind intended here is not a brutal imposition, but the creation of an independence of authority through coming to share concepts and apply the same impersonal procedures of validation as those of the teacher. Such a liberalized kind of teaching does not just tell, though it has a place for that too. It questions, discusses, sets tasks, hints, preserves judicious silences, prompts, provokes, invites contradiction, feigns ignorance, poses problems, demonstrates, pretends perplexity, comments, explains and so on through the battery of devices by means of which passivity in intellectual learning may be overcome and a more critical learning stimulated. And as it succeeds, so independence of the teacher is gained and more and more valuable self-direction becomes possible.

Such teaching may well begin with the child's actual experience. But what of the discontinuity in concepts? It is overcome in the ambiguity of 'sameness'. For teacher and child address themselves to the 'same' thing, but each sees it differently, and the teacher redescribes 'it' in such a way as to bring the child's conceptions into harmony with his own. At the beginning, 'graph', 'rainbow' and 'Domesday Book' are only ambiguously the 'same' concrete thing, for to the teacher they are theoretical concepts but to the child perceptual or practical. The teacher, by a judicious selection from among the range of devices above mentioned, does not just transmit a piece of information, or enunciate sentences to be memorized, but *transforms* the child's concepts and therefore his experience, thus raising quite new questions to be asked.

The reaction of the 1931 Report against the verbalism which resulted from a failure to start from the concrete was absolutely right in that much. What in the event has not been so clearly seen is the necessity still of teaching, especially at the junior stage. The demand to start from the concrete can be made compatible with this necessity only on some such methodological principle as that of 'redescription of the concrete', which is now suggested to overcome the discontinuity earlier discussed. The child must repeat, now at a higher and more sophisticated level, what he earlier managed largely by himself in coming to see a bulky shape as a table.

But what about motivation? First, let us note that there seems no alternative to such a methodological principle, so that we do not really have a choice here if children are indeed to enter into their intellectual inheritance. It is interesting to note in passing that even in nursery and infant schools 'good teachers' give a massive amount of incidental instruction (Gardner and Cass, 1965, 35 and 38).

Secondly, why should it be assumed that three of our greatest cultural achievements, namely mathematics, science and history, must be boring? Doubtless it is an idle dream to suppose that the way to an education could lie up an unbroken gradient of ever more fascinating activities. But, given a readiness on the part of the teacher to vary his approach, and given a just allocation of materials, there would seem to be no reason why some flicker, or more, of intrinsic motivation should not be generated, even in the most ignoble of surroundings. In any case, 'the fresh intelligence which nature so plentifully supplies in each generation has a right to be endowed with intellect' (Barzun, 1959, 259).

Chapter Seven

ACTIVITY, SELF-EXPRESSION AND THE ARTS

THE CONCEPT OF A HUMAN ACTIVITY

'The curriculum is to be thought of in terms of activity and experience'. But what is the relationship, if any, between experience and activity? Might the one rather than the other be the more particular concern of the primary school? And what could be meant by 'activity methods' in teaching? Before even attempting an answer to any of these questions, it would be useful to try to get a firmer grip on the concept of activity itself; for a human activity is not just, nor indeed even necessarily, a movement of the body.

This is evident from the fact that any bodily movement is compatible with very various activity-descriptions. To take the usual case, if I see an arm waving, the relevant activity may be beckoning, warning, taking some physical exercise, directing traffic and so on. Even quite contrary activity-descriptions may be compatible with the same set of movements. A man seen writing his signature on a piece of paper may be either issuing a death-warrant or issuing a reprieve. But the palm for illustrating this point must go to A. J. Ayer, who says, of raising and drinking a glass of wine, that it could conceivably be described as

an act of self-indulgence, an expression of politeness, a proof of alcoholism, a manifestation of loyalty, a gesture of despair, an attempt at suicide, the performance of a social rite, a religious communication, an attempt to summon up one's courage, an attempt to seduce or corrupt another person, the sealing of a bargain, a display of professional expertise . . . an act of expiation, the response to a challenge . . . *Etcetera* (Ayer, 1964, 7–8).

All human activities, even the most grossly physical, are necessarily mental activities. By 'mental' here is not intended that idiom in which we speak of things as being 'done in the head', like mental arithmetic. What is meant is that activities necessarily involve *consciousness* of what one is doing, and also, as was seen in connection with play and reality, consciousness of one's situation apprehended under some description. In a sense, each of us is therefore the 'final authority' on what he is doing, though certainly in the face of some strange behaviour we should feel confident in calling a man mad, or hallucinated, because his behaviour was quite unintelligible to us. The matter could be pursued further if one wished to pursue it by asking such questions as how a smile can be enigmatic, or how deception is possible.

The meaning of what people do, the correct description of their activities, becomes more and more transparent to us as we come to understand a form of social life and come to learn its public language. An activity such as 'telephoning' is at first understood by a baby largely in terms of perceptual concepts. 'Telephoning' is getting hold of an object of a certain colour, shape and size, placing it somewhere in the region of one's shoulder, and at the same time burbling into the air. Only with the attainment of a proper practical concept of a telephone does he see it as an instrument with which to communicate with others situated at some distance. Or consider P. Winch's case of 'voting' (Winch, 1958, 51). Does the tribal African who marks the slip and places it in the box 'vote'? In a certain minimal sense of course he does, but the concept of voting is of an operation given a meaning in terms of elaborate political institutions, and of procedures for choosing political representatives. Without that understanding, 'voting' approximates to the baby's 'telephoning'.

A baby in the midst of the family's activities nevertheless remains excluded from them. No-one hides anything, but he cannot see what is going on. He has to acquire an understanding of domestic life before he can grasp what is there and open for all to see going on around him. Later, the transparent obviousness of it all will be shaken only with difficulty, as it may be, for example, if we are asked to describe in a court of law what we 'actually' saw of some incident, without giving the court our 'interpretations' of the event. The supposed obviousness of what a person is doing is also put in question when children play the games of guessing what another person is miming, and of 'follow the leader'.

Consider a new student teacher sent on an 'observation' to a school. What will he 'observe'? His experience and developed social understanding will reveal to him the meaning of the apparatus and of much of the activity of the teacher and the children in the class. But is that everything? In this case the answer will depend very much on his knowledge of the appropriate theoretical concepts of psychology, sociology, history and philosophy, and of the subject that is being taught. In this dependence on having an appropriate piece of theory lies also the danger of external imitators of reform, and of unjust critics of change. For they see the 'externals', but lack the theoretical concepts which alone give a grasp of the meaning. The desks are rearranged from rows into groups, 'because it's all groups now', but the class teaching continues, with twisted necks and general discomfort as the result. The old-timer rejects the 'college' ideas, because all he can see is the bustle, and all he can hear is the noise.

All human activities are *mental*, but their meaning only becomes transparent as we come to understand a form of social life and the concepts developed by its communities of theoretical inquirers. Hence the hostility to Behaviourism, for here, highly ambiguous as between activity and bodily movement as 'behaviour' is, human activities are apparently being redescribed in a way which leaves out their meaning to the agent, and which reduces them to reflexes, twitches, jerks, 'responses', 'shaped' response-sequences and organismic activity to be 'reinforced' on some appropriate 'schedule'. Language becomes 'verbal behaviour' and mind an 'intervening variable'. Thus the human person is, as it were, thrust outside of the experimenter's community of like-minded agents and is replaced by an object. This could be a useful thing to do in relation to certain legitimate experimental purposes and in relation to certain treatments. Surgeons, physiologists, lift-designers and those who determine an aeroplane's permissible passenger load all regard people as objects, and very appropriately.

Behaviouristic spectacles would become pernicious only if they became contact lenses, and if instead of treating people as objects for some specific purpose, within a wider awareness that they are really people all the time, the Behaviourist actually came to see people *as* organisms, without qualification. He would then no longer simply be a methodological Behaviourist, whose methods may indeed have their uses in the service of ethical human life, but would have become a metaphysical Behaviourist, no longer believing that there are such things as persons and minds. How people's activities appeared to themselves, the ways in which they gave meaning to their lives, would be considerations which were no longer of any concern to him.

As a final illustration of these points to do with mind, meaning and human activity, consider reading. Could a Behaviouristically minded psychologist teach babies to read, as some of them, such as Doman, claim to be able to do? If we agree that reading is not *just* word recognition, but an activity in which we grasp an appropriate level of meaning from a text, then whatever responses a child might make, he cannot be said to be 'reading' until he is grasping meaning. This in turn requires some degree of mastery of a language. Thus among the 'readiness' conditions for reading there are, as it was pointed out earlier in chapter three, *conceptual* conditions too. One cannot, therefore, teach a child to 'read' before he has some mastery of language. Even with a child who can read, doing a test such as Schonell's word-recognition test may embrace very different sorts of activity within the range of what is conventionally scored as 'correct'. Word-recognition may shade into guessing and correct sound-blendings, with the child taking it only on trust that these are indeed meaningful words that we require him to utter (see Dearden, 1967a, section 2).

Then what, to return to our original question, is the relationship between experience and activity? The description of a human activity has to make intelligible two things: (i) the situation in which the person sees himself as acting, which includes the circumstances in which he acts and the foreseen consequences of so acting; (ii) the inclinations or values which furnish him with reasons for acting, and for exercising his capacity to do this or that at will. Activity-descriptions answer the question 'what is so-and-so doing?' But of course they do not exhaust the description of conscious life, because there are things that affect or even afflict us as well as things that we do, such as sensations, emotions and moods, none of which is an activity.

Experience and activity, then, cannot be divorced. On the one hand, thinking and conceptualizing are themselves activities, things which we do, get correct or incorrect, improve upon or rest content with. On the other hand activities are unintelligible apart from an understanding of the situation, or apart from the beliefs about that situation in terms of which desires are weighed in deliberation, and plans, policies and projects for the future are formed. Of course, physical and practical activities, such as football and cooking, can be contrasted with theoretical activities, such as solving equations, testing hypotheses and sifting through archives, but all are activities and all are mental. Again, the practical may instigate the theoretical, and the theoretical illuminate the practical. There is even a 'theory of games' now. Thus mind is not an agency which springs into action only when lips are sealed, or when books are opened, but is operative throughout the range of human activity, covert or otherwise. That is not to say of course that every aspect of mind, or every kind of concept, enters into every activity (see Hampshire, 1959, passim).

ACTIVITY, LEARNING AND 'ACTIVITY METHODS'

'The curriculum is to be thought of in terms of activity and experience rather than of knowledge to be acquired and facts to be stored.' What, then, should a teacher actually do to get some 'activity' going? J. Barzun writes of classrooms where 'noise and agitation reach their educative peak' (Barzun, 1959, 109). Is that what is meant? There can be few dark corners of the theory of primary education as badly in need as this one of some of Plowden's 'astringent intellectual scrutiny'. In entering it, one makes a Platonic descent down into the cave. Ever since 1931, disclaimers and qualifications have been appearing to correct 'false' views of what activity is. Is it somehow opposed to acquiring knowledge, for example? 'A word of caution, however, is needed here. To emphasize activity and experience is not to belittle the value of the knowledge that they bring. Indeed, unless they bring knowledge that will serve present and future needs, experience and activity lose a great deal of their value' (H.M.S.O., 1937, 112).

Again, if children's activities are to be the centre of the curriculum, then does teaching go out? 'It is a pity that there has been so much misunderstanding about what has been called "activity"—and a still greater pity that it has sometimes been assumed that it and methodical teaching are mutually exclusive. It is time that the term was given a more homely and general connotation, and that the misleading assumption that the children's activity somehow excludes good teaching should be dropped' (H.M.S.O., 1959, 52).

If it does not belittle knowledge, and it does not exclude good teaching, is it simply that there should be more physical movement, more getting up and moving about? One might suppose so, for 'a sedentary life is exceedingly unnatural for a child of infant school age' (H.M.S.O., 1933, para. 89). Nevertheless, there may be misunderstanding here too, for activity 'should not be taken to imply that the child should always be physically active, always bustling about, always "doing", always manipulating; thought itself is activity, and in this sense the child may be most active at times when he is perfectly still and quiet' (H.M.S.O., 1965, 60). But if *this* is so, how is 'activity' something different in character from teaching and learning in the elementary tradition? Children in the elementary school certainly were often perfectly still and quiet. And are not copying blackboard notes, reading round the class and doing 'comprehension' exercises activities, in any 'homely and general connotation'?

'A teacher was asked by an inspector to provide more activity for the children. "I don't know what you mean", she replied, "they are always doing something: reading, singing, or writing" ' (Boyce, 1945, 9). Miss Boyce then goes on to explain that the activity the inspector was asking for was *child* activity. But 'child' activity is not, as a homely and general person might suppose, just whatever children do, but 'that kind of activity in which the child wishes to engage, and not that which is dictated to him by any adult' (op cit., 5). But then, would it not be child activity if the child wished to be taught arithmetic, or to have a geography lesson?

It can be seen in this reference to 'child' activity, however, and in such a statement as that 'the point of "active" lies in the seeking behaviour of the subject' (Brearley and Hitchfield, 1966, 163), that 'activity' is a variant on the child-centred doctrines of need, interest and growth that were discussed in chapters two and three. This becomes still clearer in an article by Miss M. Bradley, who explains that 'activity methods' constitute a flexible approach to teaching based on three principles: (i) interest, which 'arises from the impact of what is outside upon our impulses', and which leads to improved attitudes to oneself, to life and to learning; (ii) wholeness of growth (for example, social learning should not be neglected); (iii) experience (Bradley, 1950, ch. 2).

It is not, therefore, simply that there should be activity in the classroom, since it would be quite impossible to exclude that anyway. It is rather that there should be a special kind of activity. And one can now see that in using the general concept of a human activity to recommend just one very particular *kind* of activity, strongly to be contrasted with other kinds, confusion and muddle were inevitable. Furthermore, one can also now see that activity theorists are involved in the more general error of thinking that procedural recommendations about *how* things should be done can be substitutes for, and not just supplements to, a careful statement of curricular aims.

In at least one case, however, the omission of attention to curricular aims in favour of talk about procedural principles has apparently been remedied by carrying over 'activity' into the curricular field and trying to set up a curriculum in term of kinds of activity. Thus Miss M. V. Daniel sets out seven categories of activity into which her suggested curriculum falls: physical, environmental, constructional, creative, imaginative, tool subjects and the school setting (Daniel, 1947, 83–4). But upon what principle is this division made? For unless it is based on some reasonably clear principle we are merely being set the problem of locating the familiar in an idiosyncratic maze of new categories. One cannot forbear remarking here how often books and reports on primary education offer some general exhortatory talk and some jibes at 'subjects', with their 'arbitrariness' and 'watertightness', only to follow this, after some transitional excuses, with a discussion of the usual range of avowedly detested subjects. But does not Miss Daniel's scheme escape such grounds for criticism?

A valuable exercise is to try to guess what each of her categories might include before actually looking to see. One should be able to do this if there really is a principle here. One might expect, therefore, 'imaginative activities' to include literature and drama, as indeed it does, but why are the other aesthetic subjects divided off into a separate class called 'creative activities'? Is this not just a distinction without there being any real difference? Apparently not, because to Miss Daniel history, geography and religious knowledge are also 'imaginative activities'. In that case, should not science be included too? Answer: no, because science is a 'constructional activity', which belongs with handwork. After this last revelation the reader may be left to imagine, or to create, or to construct what the 'school setting activities' would be. Even 'physical activities' contains some surprises, such as rest, and meals. The *coup de grâce* to activity as a curriculum concept, however, is unwittingly delivered by those infant teachers who make it into yet another subject, alongside the rest.

Let us try again, and patiently attempt a reconstruction out of this sorry mess which the activity theory has produced. Our concept of a human activity, it was argued, is such that activity cannot be equated with bodily movement and may not even involve it, but on the other hand every activity is 'mental', in the sense that it involves consciousness of what one is doing. The distinction of physical, practical and theoretical activities is therefore a distinction of kinds within a general class. It is not a distinction between 'activities', taken to be overt, and something else, not activity, which is concealed or covert. Next, activity cannot be divorced from knowledge or belief. There must be beliefs about one's situation and also beliefs in terms of which desires are elaborated and consequences drawn for there to be activity at all, rather than just twitching, jerking or thrashing about.

Again, activity may be free or unfree, valuable or worthless. Soldiers doing drill under the sergeant's orders and children copying down the capes and bays of France, if such ever happened, would all be engaged in activities. Such a concept is therefore far too general and permissive to sum up an educational programme. Furthermore, since being educated is a matter of learning various things, whether by oneself or by being taught, it is kinds of learning that a curriculum should set up as aims.

Here a broad distinction might be made between 'learning that', 'learning how to', and 'learning to' (Scheffler, 1960, ch. 5), or between conceptual knowledge, skills and settled dispositions. Thus one might acquire scientific knowledge, laboratory and research skills, and a disposition to be scientific about appropriate things, or one might learn about God, learn how to make conversions, and acquire a worshipful disposition. It is important, as Scheffler remarks, to have these distinctions clearly before one's mind in curricular discussions about 'teaching science', or 'teaching religion', because one of these three modes of learning might be acceptable when others were not, as indeed has been argued to be the case in this book concerning religion.

It has been argued at length in chapter four that the first of these three modes of learning, the one concerning conceptual knowledge or 'learning that', is fundamental from the point of view of curriculum construction. Skills and dispositions are manifested in activities, but activities presuppose knowledge and beliefs about one's situation and what one might choose to do in that situation. Even if one thinks, not so much in terms of the basic kinds of understanding which mark out the aims of education, but in terms of the growth of understanding from concrete to abstract, for which purpose perceptual, practical and theoretical concepts were distinguished, still it is in terms of conceptual learning that one best finds one's bearings. Nor is this in any way to depreciate emotion, activity, skills and dispositions, or to say that understanding must come *first in time*, or first be perfected, before anyone can feel or do anything. It is, however, to make clear a basic condition of and ingredient in any feeling or doing at all.

If we now return to activity methods, two acceptable senses can be given to the phrase. First, there could be teaching methods especially appropriate to the learning of perceptual and practical concepts. These methods might well indicate the desirability of activities such as play and free investigation within a carefully structured environment, with such care being exercised over the selection of materials and such interventions being made as are necessary to secure an educational function to these activities. This, one judges, would be an appropriate teaching method in the nursery school, and, to a varying degree for different children in different parts of the curriculum, in the infant and even lower junior school.

This in fact seems to be what activity-theorists have often been meaning to say. There is a constant scattered recurrence in their writings of such notions as 'concrete experience', 'own interests', 'natural growth' and 'freedom to choose'. The 'concrete experiences' may now be identified in terms of perceptual and practical concepts, the 'interests' come in with learning, and the 'natural growth' may be taken to mark the fact that such learning is permissibly promiscuous and arises out of natural curiosity and a desire to share in the activities of others. Such learning very largely does 'just come', given the right material environment and properly qualified supervision.

But what about theoretical concepts, such as base of eight, decimal fraction, focus of ellipse, oxygen, magnetic field, cliff erosion, Viking invasion and Spanish Armada? Are these to be 'picked up' in the promiscuous rovings of natural curiosity too? Here, surely, and appropriate to this more sophisticated stage in the growth of understanding, a *second* sense must be given to 'activity methods' if the phrase is to signify a definite and acceptable methodology at all. The same notions collected from activity-theorizing, namely experience, interest, growth and autonomy, must now be given new and distinct meanings. 'Experience' may still be taken to be the concrete experience associated with the things that the teacher introduces, but these 'things' are to be redescribed by the teacher. 'Interest' may mean either an original or a newly stimulated interest in the 'things', but the teacher's long-term intention here will be to transform this into an intrinsic interest in the kinds of theoretical understanding he wishes to develop. And 'growth' will be the development of a rational autonomy.

This *second* kind of 'activity method' is therefore to be equated with the liberalized concept of teaching described in the previous chapter. Such a mode of 'teaching', in Scheffler's normative sense, is a constant stimulation to activity of mind through the encouragement of critical acceptance. Furthermore, it encourages self-directed activity, for mastery of the concepts and validation procedures of basic forms of understanding is precisely the condition of rational independence of authority. Rational autonomy is not the proliferation of private imaginings and phantasies, but the private use of public possessions. Paradoxically, one gains a well-founded independence precisely to the degree to which one enters into community.

SELF-EXPRESSION, CREATIVITY AND THE ARTS

Five basic forms of understanding were distinguished in chapter four as furnishing developmental aims in primary education. Of these, only the theoretical have so far been discussed in terms of procedures. It would therefore seem appropriate now to give some special attention to procedures in relation to aesthetic and ethical understanding, the first of which will occupy us for the rest of this chapter. The arts we shall have in mind will include drama, poetry, 'creative writing', singing, instrumental music, dancing, painting, drawing, clay modelling, carving and the like, all of which contribute in distinctive ways to the development of aesthetic understanding.

Self-expression. Two sides to aesthetic understanding need to be distinguished in considering the place of the arts in the curriculum. These are what may be called *appreciation*, as in reading poems, listening to music or looking at pictures, and *expression*, or actually producing something by one's own creative activity, as in writing a play, modelling a bird, or making a drawing. The distinction is somewhat obscured in those arts involving performance, such as singing, dance and the drama, but is clear enough for the purposes of the present limited discussion.

It could be predicted, and the prediction would be confirmed, that in the elementary tradition there would be little attention given to the arts and that that little would be very much biased towards appreciation. Little attention would be given because of the utilitarian criterion underlying the curriculum, with its stress on basic skills and 'real work'. Literature and music represented the main concession of the elementary tradition to the arts, though in both cases what was to be read, written about and sung was dictated by the teacher. Writing, or 'composition', the one allowance to the expressive side of aesthetic understanding here, was seen as an opportunity for further exercises in spelling and handwriting. It was also seen as demanding some teaching in what was taken to be 'literary', for instance the plentiful use of such words as 'verdure' and 'gambolling lambs'.

The bias towards appreciation followed from the pessimistic view of human nature. 'Self-expression' could only be construed as a holiday for the unredeemed side of children's natures. Further-more, judging children's work by adult standards inevitably found it to be grossly defective, and hence confirmed these pessimistic suspicions. This in turn justified more and more exercises, and the provision of various crutches to support the limping inadequacy of children's work.

Setting the subjects and providing 'literary words' have already been mentioned in connection with writing. Where the visual arts were concerned the teacher had to be adept at drawing on the blackboard with coloured chalks, or in providing ready painted pictures to copy or templates round which to draw, so that choice should be excluded and nature be properly confined. Such was the taint of error that even alterations, which might have indicated the beginnings of critical reappraisal, were severely frowned upon. And throughout, the time given to the arts was begrudged, the media used were severely restricted, and the opportunity for choice and doing something of one's own were, if possible, eliminated. Only work which conformed to certain uniform adult standards was generally acceptable.

Against this tradition it was very natural for child-centred theorists to react with a demand for 'self-expression' as the master method in securing 'growth'. W. Viola, for example, summed up his view of the teacher's function in relation to art by the principle 'not into the child, but from the child' (Viola, 1942, 47). Dictation and the imposition of a spurious sophistication were to be strongly resisted, crutches were to be dispensed with, and abundant opportunities were to be given for choice and doing things for oneself. This was especially the case with the visual arts, but by slow degrees also with dance, and only quite recently with writing. The self-expression reaction, however, was itself expressive of a variety of demands deriving from a variety of sources, though all of them were more or less closely connected with Romanticism.

One Romantic element was an admiration for the sincere, fresh, or genuine, even if it might be crude, unfinished or obvious. Another was the belief that in the arts, as in everything else, ability was something that just unfolded. 'The task is to let the child grow naturally, but not arbitrarily . . . To let children grow means to let them grow according to their eternal innate laws' (Cizek, quoted by Viola, 1942, 45). The 'unfolding' doctrine gained some support from a recognizable progression from scribble towards realism in the drawing of young children. Analogies between children's art and the newly discovered art of primitives were also detected. These analogies were seen as confirmation of the 'bio-genetical law' that we recapitulate in our unfolding the history of mankind, and 'we all believe in the biogenetical law' (Viola, op. cit., 18).

All of this helped to protect children's efforts from adult criticism by shrouding it in pregnant mystery, as being something of rich symbolic meaning upon which blundering adults should not intrude. Child-centred theorists who were acquainted with the history of art would justify their non-intervention by examples drawn from that history. Did not the Egyptian artists mix up front views with profiles, as with the eyes, and did not medieval artists ignore perspective, and paint lollipop trees? Then by what right are children to be 'corrected'?

To these strands in the reaction must be added psychoanalysis. Here, the Romantic view of the emotions as erupting in creative inspiration could be combined with a belief that it was positively harmful to repress these emotions. All shackles should be removed from the subterranean creative flow, if art was to be achieved and neurotic disorder avoided. As J. A. Hadfield, himself a psycho-logist, comments: 'If . . . this was true, it was natural that many amongst the public (and also amongst the educationalists, who should have known better) translated Freud's teaching to mean that we should never frustrate or discipline the child, but on the contrary should let him do exactly as he liked; otherwise we may be laying in store all kinds of neurotic disorders for his later life . . . Child Guidance Clinics therefore provided rooms where children could fling water about and be as dirty as they liked' (Hadfield, 1962, 19).

Yet if the effects of this complex reaction have been liberating for the youngest children, as indeed it might well be agreed that they have been, nevertheless its effects on children of junior age have been rather less satisfactory. As Plowden comments: 'There is often little progression, and the work of the ten-year-olds is less developed than would be expected from what is done by the sixes, sevens and eights' (Plowden Report, 1967, para. 680). Materials have been wasted and the satisfactions of achievement missed for want of teaching, though teaching of a liberalized kind. Different as theoretical and aesthetic understanding may be, they are alike in requiring systematic development.

First of all, 'self-expression' is too wide a notion to do an accurate job in picking out the aims of aesthetic education. In this respect it is like activity, and is open to similar abuses. Self-expression is to be contrasted with imposition from without as involving an exercise of choice in which we reveal our personal tastes, preferences and hence distinctive style of individual response. But its aesthetic value will depend on the degree of understanding we possess. The self-expression of an educated person is an exercise of choice implicitly or explicitly guided by reference to criteria. This is rather different from the wholly uninstructed and private acts of one who ignores or is unacquainted with his cultural inheritance.

Secondly, an important distinction has to be made between two propositions, the second of which by no means follows from the first. The propositions are: (i) where there is no opportunity for choice, there can be no aesthetic self-expression; and (ii) where there is plentiful opportunity for choice, there will be plenty of aesthetic self-expression. The first proposition is a conceptual truth about 'self-expression', but the truth of the second by no means follows from it. Opportunity for choice is only a necessary and not a sufficient condition of aesthetic self-expression.

Creativity. Perhaps the first point worth making about creativity is that it is not confined to the arts. Creative work is both possible and extremely valuable in mathematics, in the sciences and in historical writing, to take the three theoretical forms of understanding that were discussed in the previous chapter. Wherever new theories can be put forward, new proofs advanced, fresh hypotheses formulated or old knowledge reviewed, there is room for creative work. The tendency to confine creativity to the arts, or to think of the arts as being especially the domain of the creative, doubtless stems from a feature of the validation procedures for aesthetic judgement that was noted in chapter four. This is the feature that a work of art is not a discovery of something which is in a sense already 'given', even if only by implication. A work of art is a new individual and not a contribution towards the solution of a common and antecedently specifiable problem.

There are traditions in art, of course, and there are explorations of media and techniques which might almost be called 'aesthetic research', but still a distinction would seem to remain which would explain the tendency for creativity to be thought of as most noticeably to be found in the arts. It is this very same feature of art, of course, which makes 'objectivity' so difficult to secure, and the criteria for validation so difficult to state. Indeed, critics have been caught out so often in the past, as they were over Impressionism for example, in trying to lay down in advance what is or would be 'good' art, that they have now been taught a caution which may even amount to a failure to discriminate. But the difficulty of what to say when artists of demonstrated competence in traditional modes nevertheless choose to reject such traditions is surely not a problem that need afflict the primary school teacher to such a point of intimidation.

Even if one confines attention to creativity in the arts, however, important distinctions still need to be made, since at least four senses of the word are commonly found being run together. First, creativity may simply mean crude self-expression, and imply a corked bottle theory of the emotions together with a requirement that the cork be taken out, so that tensions can be relieved, exuberant release experienced, and a general euphoria of personal satisfaction be achieved. Since this sense of creativity divorces it from the evaluation of any product and makes it simply a matter of pleasurable self-feeling, indeed almost a dribbling of words and ideas, it naturally commends itself to a certain kind of 'democratic' sentiment, for all can experience it and at no trouble at all. This first sense is perhaps commonest in American writing on the subject (see Nash, 1966, ch. 7).

A second sense of creativity, and again one in which it is attributed to everybody, equates it with not falling below a certain minimal rationality in what one says and does. In this sense, the species 'man' is said to be creative, to pick out the fact that rules and standards are learned and critically followed. This was the sense of 'creativity' apparently intended by Sir Percy Nunn when he wrote that 'a man who does not write novels or plays or verse, who does not compose music or invent machines or spin scientific theories, might resolutely deny that he is ever a creator.' But the facts of speech would confute him, Nunn says. For 'the child learns speech, but his use of the idioms thus conserved and inherited cannot possibly be foreseen; even the dullest person must constantly make a novel use of them to express his needs and desires and feelings, to report what he and others have done or intend to do, and so on. All these are humble but veritable acts of creation' (Nunn, 1945, 34). No doubt what Nunn says is true, even if rather unexciting. One need only speak to be creative.

In yet a third sense, creative means 'original', which is itself far from being a clear idea. Roughly, the 'original' is what is novel or unconventional in some more or less striking way, so that the creative person will now be the one who notably departs from the usual modes and approaches. Originality is not a necessary condition of art, as witness the long history and traditional forms of Egyptian art, or the more than a hundred symphonies written by Haydn compared with Beethoven's nine. Creativity can be shown in elaborations upon and variations in a broadly fixed traditional form, as well as in radical innovation.

Originality is likely to be prized, both in the arts and throughout social life, in a society with a general expectation of progress, for innovation will be a necessary condition of important steps in such a progress. Our own culture has such a general belief in progress, especially of a technological kind. Not surprisingly, therefore, 'creative' nowadays is often equated with 'original', and marks out the person who is a possible source of new ideas in keeping a lead in the space-race, improving the product, and so on.

Aesthetic creativity, however, is neither pleasurable self-feeling, nor just speaking, nor *necessarily* being original. What it is can be determined only by reference to the aesthetic object produced, whether this 'object' be a poem, story, song, dance, painting or carving. That is to say, the criteria of creativity here will be the criteria of what is good or bad in the appropriate art. The people to assess 'creative writing', for example, will be those who have some literary discrimination, and not psychologists, unless of course, as is often not the case, the same man happens to be both. Similarly with creativity in making music, in modelling or in painting, it is the person who can make the appropriate critical judgements who will be able to recognize what is creative and what not.

If this is right, then the development of creative abilities in children will be a matter not just of unfolding in a permissive atmosphere, but of aesthetic *education*. There will be a great deal of learning to be done. Presumably this is why bold new scientific hypotheses do not spring from the minds of poets, why demonstrations of Goldbach's theorem are not offered by historians, and why plays are not produced by entomologists. Of course, a man might *learn* in more than one field of possible creativity, and perhaps even be a Leonardo, but the point still remains that he would have to do some learning.

Teaching and the arts. An important problem in the development of aesthetic understanding is the right balance between what were earlier called the appreciative and expressive sides. The problem can be more simply framed, however, by asking how much of the expressive side there is to be, since both necessarily involve understanding and appreciation. Creating a work of art is attempting to produce or perform something that is simultaneously critically appreciated. The relationship of expression to appreciation here is quite analogous to that between writing and reading, where similarly both involve reading.

There are perhaps two main grounds on which providing opportunities for expression may be defended, where the choice is not already settled by material circumstances. The first would be the personal satisfaction to be derived from doing something for oneself, with the possibility always of continuing to do it later as a constituent in one's conception of a worthwhile form of life. The second would concern both motivation and discrimination, for it may well be the case that opportunities for creative expression, especially where young children are concerned, best generate a liking for and enjoyment of the arts, and best lead to discrimination and critical judgement. A possible danger to be guarded against, however, and one currently well illustrated by poetry, is so to bias the time spent towards expression that the child's concept of what a poem might be is unduly impoverished through neglecting the much more accomplished work of others. Indeed, if poets' poems are never read and enjoyed together, what must a child be supposed to be doing in 'trying to write a poem'?

The very first stages with some of the arts must necessarily be more biased towards appreciation than towards expression. Nursery rhymes, stories and poems must first be heard, since they cannot yet be read and still less be written. Here, quite a considerable amount of teaching of the basic language skills is necessary before anything recognizably aesthetic is possible. Similarly with music, songs must be heard before they can be sung, and instrumental techniques must be acquired before music can be played, though the difficulty here can be eased by using simple instruments such as triangles and tambourines. Music, like mathematics, early involves systematic teaching, since both music and mathematics involve new worlds, structured by well defined conventions and rules of procedure.

The visual arts, such as painting, are often the least well taught, and failure to teach here may even be regarded as a virtue by child-centred theorists. Yet the visual arts are not 'natural'. There are tribes who do not recognize photographs to be representations of anything and even in our own culture young children may fail to recognize quite straightforwardly representational painting or sculpture. What is true, however, is that given materials and an indication of how to use them, young children will be happily active, and even progress through definite stages of accomplishment, all with a minimum of comment from the teacher. Comment of a sort can tactfully be made about drawing large shapes instead of producing isolated pepperings of tiny figures, but an infant teacher may justifiably refrain from criticizing people with no shoulders, sky which never comes down to the horizon, or trees that look like lollipops.

Yet just as natural curiosity needs to be endowed with intellect, so these first beginnings in the arts need the help of teaching if this initial development is to be maintained. Too often materials are distributed with no more than encouragement from the teacher, past efforts are simply repeated, or ten minutes' work leads to having 'finished' or being 'unable to think of anything more'. Children need deliberate teaching at the junior stage, and

if they are merely surrounded by attractive materials and then 'allowed to develop on their own' they fail to develop but rather repeat a performance *ad nauseam* and with diminishing effort and sincerity of feeling . . . It must be recognized that laziness and slovenliness can mar what they paint or make no less than what they do in any other field; and a sense of progression is as necessary here as in every other aspect of education (H.M.S.O., 1959, 221).

To say that deliberate teaching is necessary is not to say that the elementary school teacher, with his classroom walls adorned with forty or fifty identical paintings of a country lane or of ducks on a pond, was right. It is not to say that prescriptive models must be provided, tricks taught, or techniques always separated out for attention. And it is not *just* to say that the teacher has an inspirational function in exciting imagery. But it is to say that he must lead in introducing new materials, media and techniques, such as collage, mosaic, plaster carving, wire modelling and paper sculpture, and that he must gradually convey a more critical understanding of what is involved in the appreciation of art and in creative expression.

Finally, it is not enough simply to exhort teachers to 'be more imaginative', as if aesthetic imagination could be switched on by an act of will, or were absent only for want of trying. The deficiencies of aesthetic education in the primary school derive from a lack of in-service training and from deficiencies in the colleges, and these in turn go back to deficiencies in the schools from which the students come. Thus there is a vicious circle created by the general undervaluation of the arts. More serious attention to them in the training of primary school teachers could, however, be coupled with the more widespread employment of specialist peripatetic teachers, especially for instrumental music, and by a semi-specialist pooling of individual abilities among the staff of a school. But where some of the performative arts are concerned, such as piano playing and the ballet, it would seem that for the foreseeable future the main effort will continue to be a private one, quite outside the range of the state primary schools altogether.

Chapter Eight

MORAL EDUCATION

Of the five basic forms of understanding distinguished earlier, four have already been discussed from the standpoint of teaching procedures. It remains in this final chapter, therefore, to discuss ethical understanding from the same standpoint. Teaching procedures cannot, of course, be completely specified purely from a philosophical point of view: psychological and sociological commentaries must also be heeded in actually making practical judgements and decisions. Nevertheless, there are distinctively philosophical considerations which do have important bearings on any such practical judgement. The first and perhaps most obvious of these concerns the question of how morality is related to religion, and more specifically, the Christian religion. (On this, see Ramsey, 1966, and MacLagan, 1961.)

MORALITY AND RELIGION

There is, of course, no *one* way in which morality and religion are connected. There are many such ways, not all of them relevant to our present purpose. For example, there are historical questions to be asked about the origins of our present social morality, but such origins are no more relevant to the validity of this morality than the origin of geometry in Pythagorean mystery religion is relevant to the proof of Pythagoras' theorem. The fact that a moral rule originated at some particular time and place is logically neither here nor there if our concern is with what ought to be done now. Similarly, administrative questions to do with the *utility* of religion in curbing the inclinations of 'the masses', or of 'the populace', do not concern us. When religion is viewed by a governing class in such a purely utilitarian fashion as that, questions to do with truth or validity cease to be of any importance at all: any religion will do, so long as it 'works'.

A third connection, which is again irrelevant to our purpose but nevertheless of great topical interest, deserves mention. This concerns the reduction of religion to morality, as exemplified in R. B. Braithwaite's lecture 'An Empiricist's View of the Nature of Religious Belief' (see Ramsey, 1966, ch. 3). On this view, religion is just a picturesque and perhaps psychologically useful way of talking about being kind and loving to people, helping the other chap, etc. Thus for Braithwaite, a religious assertion is to be interpreted as 'the assertion of an intention to carry out a certain behaviour policy, subsumable under a sufficiently general principle to be a moral one, together with the implicit or explicit statement, but not the assertion, of certain stories. Neither the assertion of the intention nor the reference to the stories includes belief in its ordinary sense' (op. cit., 71). As can easily be seen, even atheists could be regarded as being 'really religious' if such a reduction were allowed. But by 'religion' in this chapter will be meant at least a belief in a transcendent being who is to be worshipped and who exists whether we believe him to exist or not. In that sense, then, can there be any morality apart from religion?

The autonomy of ethics. An immediate answer to this which has gained some acceptance amongst philosophers in recent years is that ethics is autonomous, and hence *must* be possible apart from religion. Some sort of mistake would be involved in thinking that the matter could be otherwise. But whether one accepts this thesis or not can scarcely be settled without trying to see what the thesis is. In fact, it turns out to have several forms.

First of all there is G. E. Moore's thesis that no evaluative term, such as 'good', can be *defined* in non-evaluative terms (Moore, 1903, ch. 1). That any such attempted definition must be impossible is shown by the 'open question argument', which is that if any x is suggested as being what is good, we can always ask, without being involved in a contradiction, 'but *is* x good?' An example of this definitional fallacy would be to say that 'right' just *means* 'what God commands', for it always makes sense to ask 'but is what God commands right?' Since evaluative terms can therefore be defined, if at all, only by means of other evaluative terms, then evaluative discourse may be said to be in this sense autonomous.

A second but connected form of the thesis concerns not meaning but inference. It originates in a celebrated passage in David Hume's *A Treatise of Human Nature* (1739, bk. 3, part 1, section 1). The thesis, sometimes crisply expressed as a declaration that 'you cannot get an ought from an is', says that in any inference which has an evaluation as its conclusion there must be at least one evaluative statement among the premises, or else the inference is invalid. Often, of course, it appears that an evaluative conclusion is being drawn from 'facts' alone, either because the evaluative premise is suppressed, or because it is too obvious to need stating. But unless such a premise can be supplied, the conclusion contains more than is logically warranted and hence the inference is invalid. 'God made the world, therefore we ought to do as He commands' would be an example of such a fallacious inference. Compare: 'Hitler is the *führer*, *therefore* we ought to do as he commands.' To authorize such inferences, an additional premise must be supplied. One might note that round the corner from here there lurks a problem concerning the status of the *ultimate* premises of evaluative inference. What validates them?

This question leads to yet a third form of the autonomy thesis and one which is clearest in the work of R. M. Hare, J. P. Sartre and K. R. Popper. Its purpose is to show that our actions are in no way constrained by inclinations, customary social practices, role-expectations, authorities, gods, human nature or mindless processes. We *choose* or *decide* to act in the way we do. This is autonomy of 'the will' rather than of some form of discourse, though the two are connected in the following way. When I try to decide what I ought to do, no 'facts' can determine my decision, since that would involve me in a logical fallacy (thesis two). Only if there are rules, principles or values as criteria of relevance can the fallacy be avoided and the facts be regarded as *reasons*. But what is the status of these rules, principles or values? Must I accept *them*? On the contrary, I can always put them in question, always withdraw my commitment to them, and if I do not do so it is because I *choose* not to. I am autonomous, free and hence responsible for all that I do. There can strictly be no appeal to such excuses as 'facts forced me to . . .', 'it is only human nature to . . .', 'I was told to . . .', or 'God says . . .'. My own assent must also have been present for the action to have occurred at all.

Before seeing how this thesis affects the relation of morality to religion, however, it would be as well to elaborate a little on this third form of it, since its affirmation of individual freedom and responsibility will prove to be a crux. Three points deserve brief mention. First, 'choice' is being used here in an extended or stipulative sense in which I can be said to have 'chosen' anything if I do it at will, and hence *could* choose *not* to do it. Thus I may be said to have 'chosen' a course which in fact I have never once reflected on or compared with other, rejected, alternatives. Secondly, placing supreme value on individual freedom is apt to result in the absence of any discussion at all as to what are good reasons for choosing this or that, though surely it matters how we choose only if something other than freedom itself is at stake. Sartre, for instance, was in the absurd position of completely neglecting all ordinary desires and the institutional framework that mirrors them. But totalitarian and democratic institutions alike offer us choices: whether to struggle with the secret police or go quietly, whether to gas Jews or fight the party, and so on. If the only thing that matters is *that I choose*, then there can be no complaints or preferences here. This absurdity does not show that what is being asserted is wrong, however, but only that it is insufficient.

The third point is that this exclusive stress on individual freedom of choice seems to accompany a justificationist theory of rationality, to the following effect: a belief is not rationally held unless grounds can be given for it back as far as something that is logically unassailable. Where choice and action are concerned, this inevitably leads to the conclusion that *ultimately* all our choices must be arbitrary, involving gratuitous commitments in favour of one way of life rather than another. But this confuses being *logically* questionable with actually having a good reason to question something. As a theory of rationality this is incoherent, as Popper and others have shown, for it counsels its own rejection. The assertion 'nothing is rationally held unless it can be justified' is not *itself* justified.

The valid point contained in this talk about freedom can, however, be detached from justificationism and retained if it is put in this way: to act rationally, we do not need to have grounded everything on a logically unassailable foundation, but only to hold our actions open to *serious* (as opposed to merely logically possible) criticism. We are not determined in what we do, for we could always *not* do it, but why should that launch us out into anguish in advance of actually finding good reasons to question what we do? Even then, not *everything* will be in question, since we will be doubting on a basis of other things that for the moment we accept. Everything *could* be questioned, but not everything at once, and why question at all without good reason?

Religion and autonomy. It might be said that morality is a matter of God's commands for us His creatures. These commands constitute the moral laws by which we should be governed in all that we do. But immediately there are two objections to this, the first epistemological and the second ethical. The epistemological objection concerns the difficulty of finding out what God commands. What *is* His law for us? Is it really to institute apartheid, sacrifice our son Isaac, engage in holy wars, or refuse blood transfusions, as some believe, or have believed? How do we know? The ethical objection is that even if we know, or think that we know, what God commands, why should we obey? As we have seen (thesis two), it is fallacious to argue 'God commands *x*, *therefore* I ought to do *x*'. That one has been given orders can never by itself be a sufficient reason for a responsible moral agent to do anything. To suppose that it could be was the moral error of Adolf Eichmann and others. We must, therefore, have independent moral standards by which the orders are to be judged, and hence morality must be logically *prior* to assent to God's commands, even if we know what they are.

Alternatively, however, it might be said that how one ought to conduct oneself was not so much ordered by God as shown by Him in Christ, who was the supreme exemplar and paradigm of a moral human life. But again there are epistemological and ethical objections. The epistemological objection concerns the difficulty of establishing a historically accurate narrative of the life of Christ. The search for an indisputably true account of what we are to model ourselves on has proved difficult though fascinating, and theologians are still not agreed on such crucial facts as whether Christ actually rose from the dead. And then there is the problem of finding the right theological description for the historical life.

But even if we had an account of Christ's life as a model to imitate, why should we do so? To judge such a life to be perfect *already* presupposes, as Kant pointed out, that we possess criteria by which to judge, and criteria which are valid independently of the contingency that Jesus happened most perfectly to exemplify them. Even if it were the case that only through his life were we able to realize what those criteria were, once realized they would have no logical dependence on the fact that Christ lived, or was the son of God. An atheist might assent to such criteria. In fact, however, not all of Christ's life may be so obviously deserving of imitation. Much of what he said and did seems to be intelligible only as a policy adopted in the face of an imminently expected end to the world. Stories of taking no thought for the morrow, turning the other cheek, laying up no treasure, and giving all to the poor may have a certain poetic charm, but few seriously follow them without subjecting them to interpretation. Other difficulties appear on further reflection, such as the thought that if riches are to be got rid of as being harmful, how can it be other than malicious to give them to the poor? And by now we are, of course, judging for ourselves.

There is, however, a third possible form of argument that might be used. This time the autonomy of ethics is granted, but there is nevertheless asserted to be a connection with religion in two important ways. A range of fundamental human values, such as freedom, truth, integrity and happiness, are taken for granted, so that there is no fallacious inference from the fact of God's commanding or Christ's example. Then it is asserted that religion shows us what true freedom, happiness and so on, *really are*. Religion reveals the heart's desire and discloses the way to fulfilment, lasting peace and happiness. True happiness is to be found in the worship and ultimately the company of God, while real freedom is the choice of submitting to God's will for us His creatures. Moreover, in being omniscient and omnipotent, God has such attributes as supremely fit Him to indicate the best and wisest way of life for us. Nor is this to make obedience to God's will a matter of calculating prudence, for it is not the good for *me* but for *man* that I now see. Thus religion, it might be said, articulates what in an earlier chapter we called the 'individual ideal' component in ethics.

What of social morality? Here again autonomy may be granted. Every society must, by definition, have a language and rules of behaviour, and hence must have at least *some* notion of truthfulness and justice (see Winch, 1959). Moreover, the Bible itself grants that the moral law may be known apart from revelation (Romans, II, 14–15), and the Thomist doctrine of natural law concedes that this much may be discerned by the light of natural reason. Religion is not necessary to seeing that cruelty and stealing are wrong, or that truthfulness and fidelity to promises are right. It will, of course, be necessary where specifically religious duties are concerned, such as not to blaspheme, to pray regularly, and so on, but the autonomy of social morality may be taken as granted.

Yet, consistently with a recognition of such autonomy, a dependence on religion for a certain inward significance may be asserted. This would come about through the 'superimposition' of religious on moral concepts (see Smart, 1966). Thus in the light of religious beliefs about man, God and the world, doing wrong is also a *sin*, life is not just enormously valuable but *sacred*, marriage is not just a matter of solemn promises and fidelity to them but a *sacrament*, overcoming one's inclinations is not just a matter of moral self-control but a form of *sacrifice*, and so on. Moreover, changes advantageous to morality may in various degrees derive from this superimposition, since morality is thereby solemnized and institutionally reinforced. Concrete models on which imagination can fasten are offered and we are constantly reminded, through the doctrine of the common fatherhood of God, of our duties concerning the welfare of others. Inward support is given to us through God's grace and through Christ's promise that he is with us always. How we act is no longer just a matter of private conscience, for we are not alone and we have a spiritual destiny. A disadvantage of this reinforcement, however, is a conservatism insensitive to greatly changing social circumstances.

This is an altogether more persuasive picture of how morality and religion might be related, but, much as we might wish to accept it, there are some important criticisms that have to be faced. In the first place, granting the autonomy of ethics serves only to shift the weight of criticism over to the *truth* of religious claims. Some of the objections to be raised here were earlier indicated in chapter four. Suffice it to say that a parallel autonomy thesis can also be presented in respect of beliefs as to matters of fact. How, then, are we to be satisfied of the truth of the claims which make possible this articulation of individual ideal and this superimposition of religious on moral concepts?

A second line of criticism arises if the demand for a substantiation of the truth-claims is seen as having failed. For, characteristically, an appeal is then made to *faith*. This, of course, is not to give grounds for belief at all, since if there were grounds then faith would be unnecessary. The consequent criticism is directed at the required *submission* of one's reason and will to God's mysterious ways and inscrutable judgements. Is this not an abdication of the individual's responsibility to judge for himself? Here, of course, is the crux, for moral responsibility requires that we judge God's will by our independent standards, and moral autonomy reduces the expression of His will to the status of advice. But to judge God is to deny God. If this is avoided by making it definitional that God is right, then judging whether *this* is 'God's will' is still a matter of our independent judgement, therefore not of faith, and therefore only contingently anything to do with God at all.

The conclusion to which we come, therefore, is in line with our former remarks on the teaching of religion in common public schools. Following Strawson, we distinguished between social morality and individual ideal. Social morality was argued to be a matter on which properly to insist in public education as being a basic condition of any tolerable form of social life. The matter of individual ideals, however, was argued to be much more a matter of personal choice, with the teacher's function being no more than that of disclosure of possible ideals.

It was also suggested, following Peters, that the fundamental formal principles of social morality are fairness and the considerations of people's interests, or good. Important among such interests would be not being hurt, being helped in need, respect for property, truthfulness and promise-keeping. Often, of course, morality is given particular specification in terms of the norms constitutive of social roles, such as those of teacher, motorist, father and doctor. Learning the 'moralities' of such roles, and the more general rules that lie behind them, will be an important part of moral education. To a more particular consideration of this we now turn.

MORAL EDUCATION

General concepts and particular applications. The teaching of morality is far from being a matter mainly for the school, so that moral education must be considered in a much wider context than was found necessary for theoretical and aesthetic understanding. In answer to Socrates' complaint that there seemed to be no specialists in virtue, Protagoras justly replied: 'you are spoiled, Socrates, in that all are teachers of virtue to the best of their ability, and so you think that no-one is. In the same way if you asked who teaches the

Greek language you would not find anyone' (Plato, *Protagoras*, 327e). Our own account will support the view that teaching what is good and bad, right and wrong, is indeed as non-specialist and as pervasive as the teaching of language. But the immediate problem is not only to show how intimately moral education is linked with general mental development, but also to show how general moral concepts can be taught to children who are still at a very concrete level of understanding.

A child cannot fairly be blamed for 'telling lies' before he has properly grasped the distinction between fact and what was only imagined, dreamt or wished. Much of children's early misreporting of what they or others did is not only more charitably but also more accurately seen as what is sometimes called 'romancing', rather than as deliberate lying. Again, promises can hardly be held to count for much when to-morrow and next year are equally parts of a nebulous time-to-come, of small account compared with the immediacies of present reality. Even at the infant school stage, a child's grasp of the concept of fact, and of the implications of promising, will still be shaky. Telling the truth and keeping promises are doubtless learned only if they are plainly expected, but that does not mean that there cannot be degrees of expectation appropriate to age and understanding.

From earliest babyhood, however, children are forming some notion of persons as embodied and hence as liable to be hurt. Around these notions of persons as embodied are learned such expectations as that one should not cause pain by biting, punching or kicking. Again, not causing injury to others requires a growing mindfulness of consequences picked out as relevant in terms of such general categories as those of safety and danger. Leaving the scissors here, letting off fireworks there, or calling across the road, *could* lead to so-and-so. Learning not to be rude, not to cause embarrassment by pointing at people, and not to offend others concerning their appearance, extend the notion of hurt from a person's body to his feelings and self-concept. So far as selfishness is concerned, babies are not selfish. Selfishness presupposes an awareness of the separate interests of others, which one nevertheless chooses then to neglect. It is therefore not a possible form of intentional behaviour prior to a developed awareness of others' interests and points of view.

Learning what it is to respect property is inseparable from learning the practical concepts discussed in chapter six. A child could not understand what windows, cars, gardens, shops and libraries are without also learning what people want and use these things for. This in turn involves grasping something of the standards of valuation appropriate to these objects and grasping the rules regarding their proper use. Windows, for example, are to be seen through while at the same time providing a barrier, hence they should be clean and should not be broken. Notions such as mess, dirty, spoil, break and damage are used to mark out ways of lapsing from what is properly to be expected of us in the treatment of people's things.

Learning what is right and wrong, or good and bad, are similarly inseparable from learning role-concepts. Concepts such as mother, father, doctor, shopkeeper, motorist and postman are not simply perceptual concepts, descriptive of a pattern of movements or physical relations. A father is not just a male parent, but a man who should have a particular care and concern for his children. As Melden points out, such expressions as 'a good father', 'acting like a father' and 'not being a father' would scarcely make sense if 'father' were a purely biological concept (Melden, 1959, section 9). Again, a motorist is not simply one who successfully propels a car along the road. He ought also to be mindful of the safety of his passengers and of other road-users, to have regard to the consequences of his vehicular acts in terms of possible inconvenience to others, to remain sober and to have some care for property. Another and very important role-concept to be learned is that of pupil, and conflicts may arise, here as elsewhere, over different views as to what the role of pupil ought to be. Parents and teachers do not always share the same concept here and hence a child may be faced with contrary expectations.

These examples are perhaps a sufficient illustration of how

general moral concepts are given concrete application in early moral learning, but some general points might be made in conclusion. The first point is to note the unavoidable saturation of social life by morality, and hence the gross inadequacy of equating it just with sex and charitable acts to the needy. Indeed, morality is so much interwoven with social life and mental development that it might at first sight seem impossible how there could be any ground from which to criticize and reappraise the current *mores*. Yet such a ground is provided by the formal principle of fairness and by an education which provides an enlarged and enriched view of a person's possible interests, or good.

The second general point is that there is no separate task of acquiring the concept of a *person*, as a piece of learning quite distinct from forming practical and role concepts, or such rules as those of not hurting, telling the truth and keeping promises. To grasp such concepts and rules is also necessarily to understand their anchorage in cares, concerns, interests and desires, and hence their complementarity to the existence of persons. To observe such rules is to have respect for persons. Moral life and respect for persons are, as Peters has pointed out, two sides of the same coin (Peters, 1966, ch. 8).

The third point is that in early moral learning a balance needs always to be kept between explicit mention of a concept and drawing attention to examples of it. Neither can alone be adequate if there is to be understanding. It seems often to be thought that imitation of the example of others, or coming across examples in reading, will be sufficient, but this can hardly be so. With moral concepts, as with concepts of other sorts, perception of an example already presupposes possession of the appropriate concept. How else is an example to be perceived? This difficulty emerges very clearly in the once favoured way of teaching morals through fables, such as the fable of the fox and the cheese. For how is the appropriate 'moral' to be perceived unless one already possesses the concept of vanity, flattery, or whatever? Similar considerations apply to 'doing what others do', where the difficulty is in seeing just *what* it is that others do. Even a simple game like 'follow the leader' leaves room for a misunderstanding of what others are doing.

On the other hand, teaching rules by some kind of catechism is hardly more conducive to understanding. Now the difficulty will be in making appropriate judgements. We can get a seven-year-old to chirrup 'I promise to do my duty to God and the Queen', but what would an *example* of doing such a duty be? This is surely moral verbalism. Further difficulties attaching to rules taught apart from their concrete exemplification are that they are likely to be applied rigidly, without regard to proper exceptions, and applied undiscriminatingly, without regard to degrees of seriousness as intentions and circumstances vary. The development of moral judgement is not a process in which we learn to force everything into five or six rigid categories, but a process in which we become more and more mindful of varying circumstances, easily overlooked consequences, different needs and intentions in others, and the moral rules and concepts which provide criteria of relevance and importance in all this. But granted concept and application are not separated, and are kept within the child's developing experience, then even a very general principle such as that of fairness can begin to be understood while a child is still at an early age.

Knowing how to behave. Of course, knowledge is one thing and acting upon it another. 'Knowing how to behave' is therefore a somewhat ambiguous phrase. What is necessary is not simply that children should have a conceptual grasp of such things as truth-telling, promise-keeping, hurt, property, or the obligations which go with a particular role, but that it should be natural to them to put this knowledge into practice. The possible discrepancy between action and knowledge here is, of course, one source of unreliability when research work into moral education confines itself to investigating moral judgement alone, without extending the investigation to actual behaviour.

Learning to be moral, then, is not just an intellectual matter. If it were, an acceptable form of excuse would be to say that one had *forgotten* that one should not be cruel, or that one should not steal or lie. But plainly moral obligations are not the sort of thing that can acceptably be allowed to slip the memory. Nor is learning to be moral just a matter of practised skill, or expertise in fitting means to ends. The exercise of skill, as Kant pointed out, is itself subject to moral appraisal. Again, skills are things which one can be more or less 'good at', which require exercise and at which one can get out of practice. But people are not more or less 'good at' being generous, nor can they be said to get out of practice at being honest (see Ryle, 1958). Leading children to see how they ought to behave, therefore, is only one half of moral education. The other half is to make it second nature with them to act upon what they know.

But if this 'second nature' is more than perception, yet not a practical skill, what is it? It would seem to be a disposition both to feel and to act in certain ways. Certainly an important part of moral education is to engender or kindle appropriate feelings, for morality is at least *caring* about certain things, taking them very seriously, regarding them as matters of great importance. It is not sufficient, as Kant and before him Aristotle pointed out, that we do what just happens to be in accordance with morality; we must also care about whatever it is and regard it as overriding. Many of the emotions are clearly directly involved in moral education, such as sympathy for the needs of others, horror at cruelty and deliberate lying, pride in keeping one's word, shame or guilt at having lapsed or failed in some regrettable way, and being upset at certain behaviour in others. The occurrence of such feelings is one criterion of the sincerity of our professed moral beliefs, while their absence may indicate that we do not really care about what we may profess. But being disposed to have such feelings is still not enough.

In his *Nichomachean Ethics*, Aristotle rightly says that morality is a matter of knowing what we are doing, of doing it for its own sake, and of acting from a settled disposition so to act. It is this last aspect, of settled dispositions to act, which must now concern us. A temptation here is to speak of 'habit', since the concept of habit has precisely the job of picking out kinds of action which we do regularly and more or less automatically (see Peters, 1963). Certainly there is a range of 'good habits', such as tidiness, cleanliness, table manners and so on, which together govern a substantial part of personal behaviour. But these are all things on the borderlines of morality. We rightly seek to 'reduce' them to habit, so that we can attend to other, more important topics, but where morality is concerned such mindlessness is contrary to what was said above about 'caring'.

When action has become a matter of habit, or when we do it out of sheer habit, or from force of habit, then it has ceased to be something about which we care very much. But this ought never to be the case with the more obviously moral sorts of action, such as truth-telling, keeping promises, responding to others' needs and avoiding hurting others. For there we are dealing directly with persons and ought to be mindful of what we are doing. We ought to be making discriminations, aware of circumstances, mindful of possible consequences, and so on. At the other extreme from tidiness and not picking one's nose are the intimate morality of personal relationships and the more public virtues of respect for general principles. In discerning with some sensitivity what we ought to do in love, marriage or friendship, or how some such general principle as justice is to be applied, habit would be out of place. Not only would it blinker where openness to the uniqueness of the situation is required, but it would remove much of the value from the action. We do not want our wives and friends to act as they do towards us just out of habit.

Our conclusion on habit, therefore, is that there is indeed an area of useful and specific behaviour that ought to become a matter of habit with us as soon as possible, but that with all of the more important ethical values our action should spring from caring and discrimination. Thus our analysis of the learning task of moral education closely parallels what was said, in effect, concerning the other forms of understanding. For there, too, in mathematics or art for example, one can distinguish the same three elements of knowledge, caring (intrinsic interest, appreciation) and action, the acting again ranging from good work habits, such as neatness and legibility, to the more mindful and considered activities of problem-solving and constructive thinking. There are also differences, of course, since morality concerns our relations to others, whereas these other pursuits may not.

The language in terms of which moral education at first proceeds is that of 'must' and 'don't', of being allowed, having to and being forbidden. Praise and blame, approval and disapproval, are consequent upon compliance or refusal in doing what is thus picked out and characterized as right or wrong. Such externality implies authority, in the sense of a person who has the right ultimately to insist that one act in this way and not that. Learning that punching hurts, how gardens are to be treated, what a library-user does, what truth-telling and promise-keeping are, involves discovering expectations and finding out that their fulfilment is if necessary insisted upon.

From this initial externality it would seem to follow that there *must* be three distinguishable stages in any learning to be moral: (i) premoral; (ii) conformity to others' expectations and demands; (iii) 'internalization' of moral rules and concepts. When Piaget traces these three stages in the game of marbles, from imitative physical movement to rule-conformity and then to autonomy (Piaget, 1932, ch. 1), or when Peck and Havighurst 'discover' the three stages of egoism, conformity and internalization (Peck and Havighurst, 1960), or when Kohlberg announces that he finds the same three stages in Taiwan, Turkey, Malaysia and the U.S.A. (Kohlberg, 1966), we might pause to ask whether such a sequence could even *conceivably* have been otherwise, granted that human beings learn by experience and that morality is originally a response to the encouragements and discouragements of others.

There are, of course, interesting empirical questions to ask as to when on average each stage is reached, or whether the last stage is reached at all by everyone, but the sequence would seem to follow simply from reflection on what it means to learn to be moral. What cannot be deduced in this way is the detailed content of the morality so to be learned, which may well show differences in

Taiwan and in Turkey. Nor is much indicated as to the manner in which the 'internalization' is to be conceived. The nature of this 'internalization' cannot be separated from the concept one has of the authority which insists that the various moral rules are acted upon. *Must* moral education, at least at first, be an authoritarian matter, or is a form of authority less offensive to reason and dignity conceivable?

Certainly moral education seems to present difficulties for any child-centred view of morality as a *natural* unfolding and development, for here are external demands. The child's desires suffer restriction and some of them have to be foregone out of consideration for the desires of others. Yet in a just society, integrity is to be achieved only by accepting an interpersonal appeal to moral reason as the arbiter of what one should do. This is presumably why Bradley could so confidently claim that 'self-realization' must be the realization of a *moral* self. Yet some theorists, such as Rousseau and Herbert Spencer, have believed that moral education could nevertheless be regarded as a natural process.

The key to the secret, so they thought, lies in learning from natural consequences. We do not touch the fire twice, and after cracking our head on the table we quickly learn to be more careful. This is true enough, but it has nothing to do with social morality. Persons, unlike fires and tables, may suffer from our activities in ways which would never naturally rebound upon ourselves. Learning to be moral is not learning a prudent caution in the face of a mindless but fortunately fairly predictable nature. It is learning to participate in a form of social life regulated by a system of rules and expectations.

Of course, acts have *moral* consequences, but it is a falsification of social realities to pretend that these are all one with natural happenings. If I am made to bear the consequences of deliberate lying by being disbelieved, or of selfishness by having my own complaints ignored, or of interference and general unco-operativeness by isolation, these are not inconveniences visited upon me by nature but by my fellow men. Such acts are intentional, not natural.

Their efficacy depends on their social meaning, not on natural causality. Nor is it enough simply to learn a cautious prudence in the face of them. These acts are meant to be understood in relation to moral rules and concepts which I am unreasonably failing to respect or care about. The problem of authority in moral education therefore remains.

Authoritarianism and rational authority. An inference the validity of which is to be considered in this section is as follows: (i) moral education is at first largely a matter of having to do what is insisted upon by others; (ii) therefore early moral education *must* be authoritarian in character. The substantial truth of the premise has already been accepted in the previous section, but the validity of drawing this conclusion from it will be denied. Manifestly, early moral education often is and has been authoritarian in character, as can be seen from looking at the elementary school tradition and the wider social structure at the time when that tradition was formed. But arguments have already been given in previous chapters for a theoretical and aesthetic education which breaks with that tradition. The question now is whether a similar break can be carried through in moral education. In order to show that indeed it can, and that therefore the above inference is invalid, two schematic concepts of moral education will be described, the first that of authoritarianism and the second involving a more rational exercise of authority.

Authoritarian morality is 'status-orientated'. What is or is not right is determined by certain persons who say so. One ought or ought not to do such-and-such because father says so, or because teacher says so, and father and teacher are in authority. The corresponding virtues in the learner are therefore unquestioning obedience, conscientious compliance and deference. Certain practical consequences of this may then be expected. For example, what matters above all is that the rule be obeyed. The result of this is typically a somewhat undiscriminating readiness to blame in the event of a breach of a rule. Intentions tend to be brushed aside and fair excuses ignored. Inabilities are not properly distinguished from lapses, and hence responsibility is what Piaget inaptly calls 'objective', meaning that attention is wholly taken up with the breach and blaming.

Secondly, because no reason is given for the rule, the only safe way is to maintain steady obedience, with the result that the rule is rigidly applied and variations in circumstances or degrees of importance are ignored. Kellmer-Pringle quotes a junior schoolboy who beautifully illustrates this. When asked to put in order of wickedness all the bad things he could think of, the boy headed his list with the two items 'murder' and 'shouting in the corridors' (Kellmer-Pringle, 1964). Such gross failure to discriminate is just what might be expected when the teaching of rules of behaviour is authoritarian. Another side to the inscrutability of such authority is that if obedience can come to be relied upon in response to its demands, then those demands can safely be extended to cover unfair privileges and to protect laziness. The temptation to such an abuse of trained gullibility must be very great.

Next, the motivation to obedience must derive from the impressiveness of the authority requiring it. This impressiveness may be gained in various ways, none of which can be connected with the point of the rule since this is not revealed. They may include generating a diffused sense of environmental threat or danger, the invocation of various kinds of bogeymen, and a readiness to characterize unfortunate natural happenings as conspiratorial with the workings of authority. Diversion of the source of motivation from the value of the rule to the impressiveness of authority may, however, make obedience liable to lapse in its absence, and hence necessitates a ready use of punishment as retribution for any such detected lapses.

Again, if an authoritarian moral education is successful, the result is far from being a person having a moral integrity based on reason, but is rather an 'internalization' of demands which is dissociated from the 'I'. Such as 'superego' is not subject to reflective criticism, and is therefore liable to uncontrolled projection and to being a source of uncontrollable anxieties. The rules being thus placed beyond criticism are regarded as sacrosanct and untouchable, and those who do not share this impression are regarded as being an evil and threatening disturbance, if possible to be suppressed. Rules may thus be perpetuated long after they have lost their point, and morality's not being a matter of *my* interests alone may be generalized into the view that it is not a matter of *anyone's* interests. It will become a transcendental matter, somehow 'in the nature of things', and beyond the wit of a 'merely human' understanding to grasp.

Yet authoritarianism is fundamentally insecure against a possible realization of its nature. For should it occur to anyone to question the demands made and the rules insisted upon, structural collapse is imminent, or else resort must be had to open force. Questioning is by implication an assertion of personal autonomy, of one's dignity as an individual, and hence one's fitness to be given good reasons in order to gain one's compliance. This intimate connection between reason, autonomy, equality and dignity has been several times mentioned already.

Such a realization makes the fictive impressiveness of the authoritarian difficult to sustain. Once questioning gets under way the spell is broken and the images are scattered. For it is then seen to be a straight and obvious fallacy to cite *his* personal demands as reason why *I* should do anything at all. To gain my compliance, he must submit to shared and public criteria of what is to count as a good reason, such as the formal principles of fairness and the consideration of interests. The presentation of, listening to and the criticism of reasons are, as Popper rightly observes, bound up with an acceptance of the 'rational unity of mankind' (Popper, 1962, ch. 24).

Yet: 'moral education is at first largely a matter of having to do what is insisted upon by others'. This was accepted as being a true statement of how it must often be for human beings who are at first amoral and who learn morality from others. How then can authority be exercised without involving a submission to authoritarianism? Two important conditions would generally have to be satisfied for the exercise of a more rational authority. The first is that there should in fact be good reasons for obliging children to do this or that. This in itself, if carried through, would typically show up a number of demands to be ungrounded in anyone's interests, or to be grounded only in unfair privileges and laziness, both of which latter adults are in a powerful position to defend.

The second general condition would be not just that there should in fact be reasons but that they should be given, so that the matter is not simply one of someone's saying so, but also one of seeing what makes it right. Expectations are to be insisted upon in conjunction with an explanation or intimation of their point. Such insistence, even contrary to a child's wishes, is not a violation of *moral* autonomy. Its basis is in mutual consideration, not in unilateral imposition. It would be sheer sentimentality, however, to suppose that 'the child is always right', or that consideration for others or a love of fairness are learned without ever reluctantly having to forego what one desires.

Furthermore, rational authority could scarcely dispense with blame, but its readiness to blame might be expected to be curbed and moderated by a greater attention to the value of necessary rules, and by the long-term aim of developing a moral autonomy grounded in reason. It ought therefore to be more disposed to inquire why lapses have occurred, and to be more mindful of intentions, fair excuses and the distinction between inability and moral lapse. Again, being mindful of the point of rules permits their intelligent application, with variations according to circumstances, and degrees of importance proportioned to seriousness. One ought to tell the truth, certainly, but being innocently mistaken is not telling a lie, and then there are tactfulness, white lies, legpulls, Santa Claus and open conflicts between truthfulness and some other kind of considerateness, as with invalids. Absolutism is gratifyingly simple and straightforward, but at the cost of rigidity, insensitivity, and an even immoral refusal to countenance the unfortunate nature of some of its consequences.

Again, rational authority insists without intimidating, and attempts to make the value of the rule a sufficient motivation to acting upon it. Because it limits its demands to what is mutually acceptable, on any fair view of all the interests concerned, it may reasonably expect greater co-operation and hence expect to be much less in need of resorting to punishment, whether corporal or of some other kind. Yet once more this is not to deny that punishment may sometimes have to be resorted to, if a sense of moral realities is to be restored and obligations are to be brought back into view. In such cases, however, the justice of punishing should be made plain by a clear characterization of the offence, so that it is not an arbitrary bolt from the blue.

The criterion of what is appropriate in the exercise of rational authority is, however, at every stage to be furnished by its aim, which is to make itself dispensable through the development of a personal moral integrity based on reason. It is this aim of achieving moral integrity which rules out intimidation, fictive impressiveness and the generation of a sense of vague environmental threat. There must, of course, always be the possibility of guilt and regret, perhaps especially for a person of integrity. To feel scruples at being unfair, inconsiderate, untruthful or dishonest is not symptomatic of a need for treatment, but one criterion of the sincerity of a moral belief. Far from being uncontrollable anxieties induced by a dissociated superego, such regrets would be the marks of a strained but continuing integrity (see Jones, 1966).

Whereas moral authoritarianism is always fundamentally insecure because of the possible realization of its nature, rational authority has no such insecurity. It is indeed an invitation to its own criticism. Again, since individual spontaneity and independence are not under the wholesale suspicion characteristic of authoritarianism, which stakes its all on obedience and sees natural impulse only as threatening a possible breach, rational authority can refrain from its own exercise in praise and welcome encouragement of any natural inclination towards fairness, considerateness, sympathy, gratitude, generosity, or any other of the finer emotions.

Three objections to this concept of rational authority must now be considered. First, what happens if the reasons for what is insisted upon cannot yet be understood? Obviously this situation is at its most acute with very young children, who may not even appreciate how they are endangering themselves, quite apart from how they are being inconsiderate of others. But to begin with, the issue can to a considerable extent be prevented from arising through simple precautions. There is no need to smack to keep a child from the fire, or to snatch from him the scissors with which he is playing, if the fire is guarded and the scissors are always put away. Unexplained interventions and frustrations of purpose can never be entirely eliminated, but they can be minimized. It might also be noted here that a child who is forbidden to do something 'because I say so', or some variant on this, is *already* a child who has grasped the appropriate language-game of giving reasons. 'Because I say so' is not a prelude to or first stage in reason-giving, but a degenerate form of it that presupposes the genuine article as the background from which it derives its sense. These earliest unexplained interventions are therefore more typically physical than verbal, or else are straight, unbacked instructions.

Next, we might well ask of some important moral rules, such as truth-telling and promise-keeping, whether it might not be better, in view of the aim, to delay insistence if what is insisted upon is not understood. Only a belief in the sinfulness of children's natures, the permanent stain on the soul of moral error and hence the necessity of early obedience to authority could justify demanding compliance with rules not yet even understood. 'Lying' then becomes a matter of 'saying naughty words', fraught with anxiety, while promises are extracted and children held to them regardless of the present insubstantiality of their intentions for the future. 'It is', as Piaget comments, 'perhaps in this domain that one realizes most keenly how immoral it can be to believe too much in morality, and how much more precious is a little humanity than all the rules in the world' (Piaget, 1932, 189). Finally, it may be replied that when rational authority and the encouragement of spontaneous considerateness are the policy, then children may be expected to be willing to take some things on trust when that trust has been built up by a manifest reasonableness elsewhere.

The second objection that might be made would be that giving children reasons invites endless quibbling, disputes and captiousness. There are two parts to the reply to this. First, it is not envisaged that life should be held up every few minutes while lengthy explanations terminating only in general rules are given. The frequent brevity of the characterizing explanation for a 'must' or a 'don't' has already been indicated in an earlier section, where illustrative and detailed exemplification was given of what it is for a child to learn respect for property, to refrain from hurting and so on. As he learns, comment becomes necessary only as the briefest of reminders. 'Stop it, you're hurting him', or 'now take your turn, that's fair', is often a quite sufficient characterization to satisfy the requirement of rational authority. Such sentences adequately convey the point, and in a way that 'I'm your father and I say you are not going out,' or 'get to bed and do as you're told', do not. Of course on some occasions a more elaborate characterization will be warranted by the importance of the situation that has arisen, as would be the case if others' toys were being maltreated, or impending just blame were being diverted onto some other innocent child, or some severe disappointment were to be borne.

But the second part of the reply to this objection is to point out that if adults cannot distinguish a dispute originating in a felt injustice from quibbling and captiousness, then they might begin to discriminate. Children, like people at any age, are in the best position to say when their purposes are being frustrated or their grievances overlooked. They are generally the best spokesmen for their own point of view. But it would be an odd child who was never cheeky, captious, or ready to abuse by quibbling the consideration extended to him. In that case, firmness and insistence would be an appropriate exercise of rational authority, since respect for the institutions and procedures of reason also has to be learned.

The third and final objection to be considered might be based on a reading of Piaget, and take the form of stating that Piaget has shown authoritarianism to be a necessary stage on the road to personal autonomy. Piaget's first two chapters, on the game of marbles and on 'moral realism', would doubtless be the basis of the objection (Piaget, 1932). Here Piaget presents the necessary three stages distinguishable in the learning of games and of moral rules as being: (i) premoral; (ii) conformity to authoritarian demands and constraints, with rules regarded as sacred and untouchable, and punishment regarded as a necessary expiation for a breach; (iii) autonomy, marked by mutuality, co-operation and discussion, with rules regarded as serving some good and punishment a way of making amends. But there are several objections to the character of this sequence if it is taken as an account of how things *must* be.

First, we have already described a coherent and conceivable alternative to authoritarianism in terms of 'rational authority'. Secondly, Piaget seems to have been unduly influenced by a contemporary interest in primitive societies, and to have read the interpretations offered of such societies into the behaviour and responses of children. He may well have been more easily able to do this because of the apparently authoritarian ethos of the social class of the children with whom he was doing his investigations. Almost immediately after the publication of his findings, Harrower failed to replicate them with middle-class children of infant school age, though comparable working-class children did confirm much in Piaget. Harrower concluded that either these three stages were not universal, or they were so accelerated that Piaget's autonomy could be found already at an age considerably earlier than he suggested (Harrower, 1934, 75–95). Indeed, the neglect of variable social influences has become a common criticism of Piaget's work, for all its valuable insights.

Thirdly, if Piaget is taken to regard his authoritarian second stage as universally necessary before autonomy can be reached, then he is so inconsistent that we can hardly believe this to be his real view. For he says that 'the earliest social relations contain the germs of co-operation . . . it is not so much a question of these successive features themselves as of the proportions in which they are present' (op. cit., 79). And again: 'there may well be something rather primitive in the relation of reciprocity, and the germs of equalitarianism may be present from the first in the relations that children have to each other' (op. cit., 283). What prevents the germs from sprouting for so long is not that they cannot do so, but that adults refuse to let them, preferring authoritarian constraint instead. Yet in his final chapter, Piaget advocates the introduction into the school of self-government, child tribunals and the other paraphernalia of classroom democracy.

Finally, if the second stage really were as authoritarian as Piaget is sometimes made to say that it must be, then it is hard to see how autonomy could ever emerge from it. Arrival at adulthood and the removal of external constraint would not result in mutuality, co-operation and discussion, which have never been shown in operation and would therefore have to blossom out of nothing; rather it would result in a dissociated internalization of the sacred and untouchable rules of which he speaks, a Freudian superego in fact.

But now, if this and the previous objections fail, then we seem entitled to return to the inference from which we started and claim that it is invalid. From the premise that moral education is at first largely a matter of having to do what is insisted upon by others, it by no means follows that it must therefore be authoritarian in character. A policy of exercising rational authority, and of giving praise and encouragement to commendable spontaneous impulses, presents a conceivable alternative more appropriate to the aim of developing a personal moral integrity based upon reason. And if conceivability is not empirical demonstration, as indeed it is not, neither has this been empirically demonstrated not to be practicable, so that its desirability is sufficient to establish a strong presumption in its favour. Furthermore, it is integral in spirit with the policy on the rest of the curriculum that has been defended in this book.

MORAL EDUCATION AND THE PRIMARY SCHOOL

The aims and general procedural principles of moral education have already been discussed in the previous two sections, but some few specific comments remain to be made without becoming involved in issues that require a good deal of empirical justification. First, if there is a moral rule or principle to be learned, it should be applied consistently. This means applying it on all relevant occasions, including those when it bears upon what the teacher himself does. It also means firmly insisting on it when spontaneity or existing dispositions are not sufficient, though such insistence should not lose sight of the values which rules ought to serve.

Secondly, a teacher must truly and accurately perceive how things are if he is to act fairly, judiciously and with some psychological insight. This involves a readiness to try to identify the less immediate reasons for the behaviour attracting his concern. Such reasons may be found in the institutional setting in which he finds he has to teach, in the family background, in individual peculiarities of reaction to himself, and so on. As well as having concern then, a teacher must, as Plowden puts it, 'retain sufficient detachment to assess what they are achieving and how they are developing' (Plowden Report, para. 873).

Again, the concern which goes along with true perception and knowledge is not happily described as love. On this point, too, Plowden is surely right in saying that 'a teacher cannot and should not give the deep, personal love that each child needs from his parents' (para. 137). His attachments are only temporary and must therefore be breakable and not creative of dependence. He must retain an impartiality in all his dealings, whereas affections alone are apt to be discriminating and partial. Furthermore, there will be some children who do not strike him as particularly lovable, and it would be self-deception dutifully to tell himself that really he loves them too. Yet his concern should certainly extend to them in an endeavour to do his best for them.

It may be said that a less emotional, more practical love,

'agapeistic love', is intended in saying that a teacher should love all his children. But little is gained by this. It always demands long explanations, and even then will be mistakenly taken for love of a more familiar and emotional kind. Sympathy, approachability, helpfulness, care, consideration for their good, and fairness, may certainly be expected as part of a teacher's professional commitment, but he cannot reasonably be required always to love every child in the classes with which he is fortuitously presented.

A further point is that the principles governing the particular arrangements and practices in a class are obviously important. Such practices as extracting forced promises, creating strong pressures towards divisive competition and cheating, urging the betrayal of loyalties to friends, restricting movement to the point that makes deception necessary to satisfy reasonable desires, encouraging tale-bearing and showing favouritism all occur, with injury to moral development that can readily be imagined. In the other direction, many practices ancillary to other curricular activities can be instituted which provide opportunities for personal responsibility to be exercised, for consideration, co-operativeness and helpfulness to be shown, and for the satisfaction to be experienced of being a trusted participant in a shared pattern of life.

A final point is that there seems little place at the primary stage for formal lessons or formal discussions on matters of social morality. For developmental reasons, on-the-spot teaching in the course of other activities would seem to be the best method. In thus confining comment to occasions as they arise, the danger of verbalism mentioned in our discussion of concept and example can more easily be avoided. A possible indirect form of teaching, strongly canvassed in the Plowden Report (para. 595), is through stories, whether fictional, historical or religious. In favour of this, it might be said that susceptibility to example is greater when children are not being directly 'got at'. Imagination and sympathy are thus extended and children come to grasp better their own experience.

Two possible drawbacks to this might be noted, however. The first relates to what was said earlier about the conceptual presuppositions of seeing something as an example. What, for instance, is a child likely to see in the story of Drake playing bowls, or the return of the Prodigal Son, if he hears no comment from others about this? Secondly, too great a reliance on the concrete has the closely related danger that restricted and even sentimental pictures may become fixed points of reference. Thus, as R. W. Hepburn comments, benevolence may be 'wholly confined to intimate personal encounters (à la Good Samaritan, the prototype), and not extended to, for example, state-planned welfare, organized famine-relief, since these are (in their details) too unlike the parable-situation. The outcome is a quite senseless prejudice against the "coldly scientific" and "impersonal" in the name of charity' (see Ramsey, 1966, 190).

Beyond these ways of contributing towards the growth of moral autonomy and the formation of active moral dispositions, there is the question of the individual's choice of ideal: the kind of person that he thinks *he* ought to be. Here, the role of the primary school would seem to be quite limited. Self-conscious searching for a personal identity and integrity begins more characteristically with the adolescent, able now and confident enough to stand over against others and custom in critical scrutiny and questioning of them. Cartesian doubt, the taking out of one's beliefs and examining of them to establish which are good and which to be rejected, is not normally a feature of the primary school child.

Yet something of a preparatory kind will properly have been going on before this stage of reflectiveness is reached. Growth in the other forms of basic understanding, in mathematics and the arts from five or so onwards, and in what begins to look like science and history from perhaps eight or nine onwards, will have begun to reveal new dimensions of the human situation, and new possibilities of worthwhile activity in the world. But the education given in the primary school is always incomplete and cannot be autonomous. Its success is to have made a good start. Which kind of start a 'good' one may be taken to be, it has been the purpose of this book to explore and discuss.

BIBLIOGRAPHY

A. *Her Majesty's Stationery Office Publications.*
BOARD OF EDUCATION (1937), *Handbook of Suggestions for Teachers.*
CENTRAL ADVISORY COUNCIL FOR EDUCATION (ENGLAND) (1967), *Children and their Primary Schools*, Vol. 1; Report. (Plowden Report.)
CONSULTATIVE COMMITTEE OF THE BOARD OF EDUCATION: (1926), *The Education of the Adolescent*; (1931, reprinted 1952), *The Primary School*; (1933), *Infant and Nursery Schools*. (The Hadow Reports.)
MINISTRY OF EDUCATION (1959), *Primary Education.*
SCOTTISH EDUCATION DEPARTMENT (1965), *Primary Education in Scotland.*

B. *Books and Articles (Pre-1900 classics are omitted)*
ADAMS, J. (1928), *Modern Developments in Educational Practice* (second edition), London: University of London Press.
AYER, A. J. (1964), *Man as a Subject for Science*, London: Athlone Press.
BARRETT, C. (1962), 'Concepts and Concept Formation' in *Proceedings of the Aristotelian Society*, Vol. LXIII, 127–44.
BARTLEY, W. W. (1964), *The Retreat to Commitment*, London: Chatto and Windus.
BARZUN, J. (1959), *The House of Intellect*, Secker and Warburg.
BLYTH, W. A. L. (1965), *English Primary Education* (2 vols.), London: Routledge and Kegan Paul.
BOYCE, E. R. (1945), *Infant School Activities* (third edition), London: Nisbet.
BRADLEY, F. H. (1927), *Ethical Studies* (second edition), London: Oxford University Press.
BRADLEY, M. H. (1950), 'Theory and Practice of Activity Methods' in *Activity Methods for Children under Eight*, ed. Sturmey. C., London: Evans Bros.
BREARLEY, M. and HITCHFIELD, E. (1966), *A Teacher's Guide to Reading Piaget*, London: Routledge and Kegan Paul.
BRUNER, J. S. (1965), 'The Act of Discovery' in *Readings in the Psychology of Cognition*, eds. Anderson, R. C. and Ausubel, D. P., New York: Holt, Rinehart and Winston.
BRUNER, J. S. (1966a), *Studies in Cognitive Growth*, New York: John Wiley.
BRUNER, J. S. (1966b), *Towards a Theory of Instruction*, Cambridge, Mass.: Harvard University Press.
CATTY, N. (1949), *Learning and Teaching in the Junior School* (third edition), London: Methuen.
COOK, H. CALDWELL (1919), *The Play Way*, London: Heinemann.
COX, E. (1966), *Changing Aims in Religious Education*, London: Routledge and Kegan Paul.

DANIEL, M. V. (1947), *Activity in the Primary School*, Oxford: Blackwell.

DEARDEN, R. F. (1966), ' "Needs" in Education' in *British Journal of Educational Studies*, Vol. XIV, No. 3, 5–17.

DEARDEN, R. F. (1967a), 'Curricular Implications of Developments in the Teaching of Reading' in *Second International Symposium on Reading: London 1965*, ed. Downing, J., London: Cassell.

DEARDEN, R. F. (1967b), 'Instruction and Learning by Discovery' in *The Concept of Education*, ed. Peters, R. S., London: Routledge and Kegan Paul.

DEWEY, J. (1916), *Democracy and Education*, New York: Macmillan.

DEWEY, J. (1938), *Experience and Education*, New York: Collier.

DEWEY, J. (1960), *Theory of the Moral Life* (reprinted from Part Two of Dewey and Tufts' *Ethics*), New York: Holt, Rinehart and Winston.

DOTTRENS, E. (1962), *The Primary School Curriculum*, Paris: U.N.E.S.C.O. (London: H.M.S.O.)

DRAY, W. (1957), *Laws and Explanation in History*, London: Oxford University Press.

FERRE, F. (1962), *Language, Logic and God*, New York: Harper and Row.

FLEW, A. G. N. and MACINTYRE, A. C. (eds.)(1955), *New Essays in Philosophical Theology*, London: S.C.M. Press.

FRIEDLANDER, B. Z. (1965), 'A Psychologist's Second Thoughts on Concepts, Curiosity, and Discovery in Teaching and Learning', in *Harvard Educational Review*, Vol. XXXV, No. 1, 18–38.

GARDNER, D. E. M. and CASS, J. E. (1965), *The Role of the Teacher in the Infant and Nursery School*, London: Pergamon Press.

GASKING, D. (1953), 'Mathematics and the World', in *Logic and Language* (Second Series), ed. Flew, A. G. N., Oxford: Blackwell.

GEACH, P. (1957), *Mental Acts*, London: Routledge and Kegan Paul.

GESELL, A. and ILG, F. L. (1943), *Infant and Child in the Culture of Today* (1965 edition), London: Hamish Hamilton.

GESELL, A. and ILG, F. L. (1946), *The Child from Five to Ten* (1965 edition), London: Hamish Hamilton.

GODDARD, N. L. (1958), *Reading in the Modern Infant School*, London: University of London Press.

GOMBRICH, E. H. (1966), *The Story of Art* (eleventh edition), London: Phaidon.

HADFIELD, J. A. (1962), *Childhood and Adolescence*, London: Penguin Books.

HALMOS, P. (1965), *The Faith of the Councellors*, London: Constable.

HAMLYN, D. W. (1967), 'The Logical and Psychological Aspects of Learning', in *The Concept of Education*, ed. Peters, R. S., London: Routledge and Kegan Paul.

HAMPSHIRE, S. N. (1959), *Thought and Action*, London: Chatto and Windus.

HARE, R. M. (1952), *The Language of Morals*, Oxford University Press.

HARROWER, M. R. (1934), 'Social Status and the Moral Development of the Child', in *British Journal of Educational Psychology*, Vol. IV, 75–95.

HEIDEGGER, M. (1927), *Being and Time* (English edition, 1962), London: S.C.M. Press.

HIRST, P. (1965), 'Liberal Education and the Nature of Knowledge', in *Philosophical Analysis and Education*, ed. Archambault, R. D., London: Routledge and Kegan Paul.

HIRST, P. (1966), 'Educational Theory', in *The Study of Education*, ed. Tibble, J. W., London: Routledge and Kegan Paul.

HIRST, P. (1967), 'The Logical and Psychological Aspects of Teaching a Subject', in *The Concept of Education*, ed. Peters, R. S., London: Routledge and Kegan Paul.

HOLMES, E. (1911), *What Is and What Might Be*, London: Constable.

HUIZINGA, J. (1944), *Homo Ludens* (English edition, 1949), London: Routledge and Kegan Paul.

ISAACS, N. (1952), 'Froebel's Educational Philosophy in 1952', in *Friedrich Froebel and English Education*, ed. Lawrence, E., London: University of London Press.

ISAACS, N. (1961), *The Growth of Understanding in the Young Child*, London: Ward Lock.

JONES, D. H. (1966), 'Freud's Theory of Moral Conscience', in *Philosophy*, Vol. XII, No. 155, 34–57.

KENNY, A. (1963), *Action, Emotion and Will*, London: Routledge and Kegan Paul.

KNIGHT, M. (1950), *William James*, London: Penguin Books.

KOHLBERG, L. (1966), 'Moral Education in the Schools: A Developmental View', in *School Review*, Vol. XXIV, No. 1, 1–30.

KOMISAR, B. P. (1961), '"Need" and the Needs-Curriculum', in *Language and Concepts in Education*, eds. Smith, B. O. and Ennis, R. H., Chicago: Rand McNally.

LOWENFELD, M. (1935), *Play in Childhood*, London: Gollancz.

LYNN, R. (1963), 'Reading Readiness and the Perceptual Abilities of Young Children', in *Educational Research*, Vol. VI, No. 1, 10–15.

MACINTYRE, A. C. (1967), *Secularization and Moral Change*, London: Oxford University Press.

MACLAGAN, W. G. (1961), *The Theological Frontier of Ethics*, London: George Allen and Unwin.

MANNHEIM, K. and STEWART, W. A. C. (1962), *An Introduction to the Sociology of Education*, London: Routledge and Kegan Paul.

MASLOW. A. (1955), 'Deficiency Motivation and Growth Motivation', in *Nebraska Symposium on Motivation*, ed. Jones, M. R., University of Nebraska Press.

MELDEN, A. I. (1959), *Rights and Right Conduct*, Oxford: Blackwell.

MELDEN, A. I. (1961), *Free Action*, London: Routledge and Kegan Paul.

MITCHELL, B. (ed.) (1957), *Faith and Logic*, London: George Allen and Unwin.

MOORE, G. E. (1903), *Principia Ethica*, London: Cambridge University Press.

NASH, P. (1966), *Authority and Freedom in Education*, New York: John Wiley.

NUNN, T. P. (1945), *Education: Its Data and First Principles* (third edition), London: Arnold.

OAKESHOTT, M. (1967), 'Learning and Teaching', in *The Concept of Education*, ed. Peters, R. S., London: Routledge and Kegan Paul.

O'CONNOR, D. J. (1957), *An Introduction to the Philosophy of Education*, London: Routledge and Kegan Paul.

OPIE, I. and OPIE, P. (1959), *Lore and Language of Schoolchildren*, Oxford: Clarendon Press.

PECK, R. F. and HAVIGHURST, R. J. (1960), *The Psychology of Character Development*, New York: John Wiley.

PERRY, L. R. (1966), 'Objective and Practical History', in *Proceedings of the Philosophy of Education Society*, Annual Conference, 1966.

PETERS, R. S. (1958), *The Concept of Motivation*, London: Routledge and Kegan Paul.

PETERS, R. S. (1961), 'Emotions and the Category of Passivity', in *Proceedings of the Aristotelian Society*, Vol. LXII, 117–42.

PETERS, R. S. (1963), 'Reason and Habit: The Paradox of Moral Education' in *Moral Education in a Changing Society*, ed. Niblett, W. R., London: Faber.

PETERS, R. S. (1964a), *Education as Initiation*, London: Evans Bros.

PETERS, R. S. (1964b), ' "Mental Health" as an Educational Aim', in *Aims in Education*, ed. Hollins, T. H. B., Manchester: University Press.

PETERS, R. S. (1966), *Ethics and Education*, London: George Allen and Unwin.

PHENIX, P. H. (1964), 'The Architectonics of Knowledge', in *Education and the Structure of Knowledge*, ed. Elam, S., Chicago: Rand McNally.

PIAGET, J. (1932), *The Moral Judgement of the Child*, London: Routledge and Kegan Paul.

PICKARD, P. M. (1965), *The Activity of Children*, London: Longmans.

POLANYI, M. (1958), *Personal Knowledge*, London: Routledge and Kegan Paul.

POPPER, K. R. (1962), *The Open Society and Its Enemies* (fourth edition, 2 vols.), London: Routledge and Kegan Paul.

PRIESTMAN, O. B. (1952), 'The Influence of Froebel on the Independent Preparatory Schools of Today', in *Friedrich Froebel and English Education*, ed. Lawrence, E., London: University of London Press.

PRINGLE, M. L. K. and EDWARDS, J. B. (1964), 'Some Moral Concepts and Judgements of Junior School Children', in *British Journal of Social and Clinical Psychology*, Vol. III, 196–295.

RAMSEY, I. T. (ed.) (1966), *Christian Ethics and Contemporary Philosophy*, London: S.C.M. Press.

RIESMAN, D. (1950), *The Lonely Crowd*, New Haven: Yale University Press.

RUSSELL, B. (1948), *Human Knowledge*, London: George Allen and Unwin.

RYLE, G. (1958), 'On Forgetting the Difference between Right and Wrong', in *Essays in Moral Philosophy*, ed. Melden, A. I., Seattle: University of Washington Press.

SARTRE, J. P. (1943), *Being and Nothingness* (English edition, 1957), London: Methuen.

SARTRE, J. P. (1960), *The Problem of Method* (English edition, 1963), London: Methuen.

SCHEFFLER, I. (1960), *The Language of Education*, Oxford: Blackwell.

SCHEFFLER, I. (1967), 'Philosophical Models of Teaching', in *The Concept of Education*, ed. Peters, R. S., London: Routledge and Kegan Paul.

SMART, N. (1964), *Philosophers and Religious Truth*, London: S.C.M. Press.

SMART, N. (1966), 'Gods, Bliss and Morality', in *Christian Ethics and Contemporary Philosophy*, ed. Ramsey, I. T., London: S.C.M. Press.

STOLNITZ, J. (1960), *Aesthetics and Philosophy of Art Criticism*, Boston: Houghton Mifflin.

STRAWSON, P. F. (1959), *Individuals*, London: Methuen.

STRAWSON, P. F. (1966), 'Social Morality and Individual Ideal', in *Christian Ethics and Contemporary Philosophy*, ed. Ramsey, I. T., London: S.C.M. Press.

VIOLA, W. (1942), *Child Art*, London: University of London Press.

WALLER, W. (1932), *The Sociology of Teaching*, New York: John Wiley.

WALSH, W. (1951), *An Introduction to the Philosophy of History*, London: Hutchinson.

WARNOCK, M. (1957), 'The Justification of Emotions', in *Proceedings of the Aristotelian Society (Supplementary Volume)*, Vol. XXXI, 43–58.

WERTHEIMER, M. (1945), *Productive Thinking*, New York: Harper and Row.

WHITE, A. R. (1964), *Attention*, Oxford: Blackwell.

WHITE, J. P. (1967), 'Indoctrination', in *The Concept of Education*, ed. Peters, R. S., London: Routledge and Kegan Paul.

WILLIAMS, B. A. O. (1965), *Morality and the Emotions*, inaugural lecture published by Bedford College, University of London.

WINCH, P. (1958), *The Idea of a Social Science*, London: Routledge and Kegan Paul.

WINCH, P. (1959), 'Nature and Convention' in *Proceedings of the Aristotelian Society*, Vol. IX, 231–52.

WITTGENSTEIN, L. (1921), *Tractatus Logico-Philosophicus* (English edition, 1961), London: Routledge and Kegan Paul.

WITTGENSTEIN, L. (1953), *Philosophical Investigations*, Oxford: Blackwell.

YOUNG, P. T. (1943), *Emotions in Man and Animal*, New York: John Wiley.

SUGGESTIONS FOR FURTHER READING

A. *Recent works in the philosophy of education*

ARCHAMBAULT, R. D. (ed.), *Philosophical Analysis and Education*, London: Routledge and Kegan Paul, 1965.

A collection of articles by nine different contributors. The articles by L. R. Perry, R. S. Peters and P. H. Hirst are closest to the interests of the present book and are entitled 'What is an Educational Situation?', 'Education as Initiation' and 'Liberal Education and the Nature of Knowledge', respectively.

O'CONNOR, D. J., *An Introduction to the Philosophy of Education*, London: Routledge and Kegan Paul, 1957, now in paperback.

More of an introduction to philosophical ways of thinking for students of education than a work wholeheartedly devoted to the philosophy of education, but a very stimulating, short introduction for anyone new to philosophy.

PETERS, R. S. (ed.), *The Concept of Education*, London: Routledge and Kegan Paul, 1967.

A collection of a dozen articles by eleven different contributors on varied aspects of teaching and learning. Several of the articles in this volume have been referred to as sources in writing the present book.

PETERS, R. S., *Ethics and Education*, London: George Allen and Unwin, 1966.

A major comprehensive work in the philosophy of education. Part One deals with the concept 'education', Part Two with the ethical foundations of education and Part Three with education and social control.

PRICE, K., *Education and Philosophical Thought*, Boston: Allyn and Bacon, 1962.

An attempt to produce a history of educational theories which reflects the critical approach of contemporary philosophy. The logically distinct components in the educational theories of Plato, Quintilian, St. Augustine, Comenius, Locke, Rousseau, Kant, J. S. Mill and Dewey are separated out. Selected extracts from the original are also provided.

REID, L. A., *Philosophy and Education*, London: Heinemann, 1962.

An introduction to the philosophy of education which discusses problems relevant to a professional course for intending teachers. Values, theory and practice, freedom and discipline, teaching and the concept of a person are among the topics discussed.

SCHEFFLER, I. (ed.), *Philosophy and Education* (second edition), Boston:
Allyn and Bacon, 1966.

This is a valuable collection of seventeen articles on concepts of education,
the study of education, teaching, intellect and skill, moral education
(four very useful articles) and education in relation to religion and politics.
Contributors are both British and American.

B. *Some important recent works in general philosophy*

BENN, S. I. and PETERS, R. S., *Social Principles and the Democratic State*,
London: George Allen and Unwin, 1959.

A modern introduction to social philosophy. Part One concerns society,
its rules and their validity, Part Two deals with social principles and
their implementation, while Part Three discusses principles of associa-
tion and the democratic state.

HAMPSHIRE, S., *Thought and Action*, London: Chatto and Windus, 1959.

An essay revolving round persons and their situation. Intention,
action, consciousness and self-criticism are discussed together in long
argument which is difficult on first reading but which offers many
rewarding insights.

MACINTYRE, A. C., *A Short History of Ethics*, London: Routledge and
Kegan Paul, 1965.

A critical introduction to the history of ethics, from the Greeks to the
present day. This is a stimulating work in a field which supplies the
background of values and morality to many educational problems. A
more general introduction to the history of philosophy is usefully
provided by the series of Pelican books edited by A. J. Ayer.

RYLE, G., *The Concept of Mind*, London: Hutchinson, 1949, paperback by
Penguin Books.

A major classic in the philosophy of mind, discussing such topics as
knowledge, will, emotion, sensation, imagination and intellect, and
presenting a sustained attack on Descartes' 'myth'. Anyone interested
in the philosophy of mind could well follow up Ryle by reading some
of the monographs in Routledge and Kegan Paul's series *Studies in
Philosophical Psychology*, edited by R. F. Holland.

STRAWSON, P. F., *Individuals*, London: Methuen, 1959, paperback edn.
1964.

An essay in descriptive metaphysics which has proved to be a classic.
The argument tries to show how bodies and persons must necessarily
be the basic particulars in our conceptual scheme as it is, though a
possible alternative scheme is explored in chapter two. Anyone new to
philosophy, however, is likely to find this a difficult book.

INDEX